ADHD Parenting:

A Beginner's Guide on Raising Boys with ADHD

Mindfulness Strategies and Modern Techniques for Parents: Make ADHD Boys Feel Loved and Supported

Eunice Churchill

Table of Contents

Introduction 1

Chapter 1 Understanding ADHD 9

The most common kinds of ADHD 10
Risk factors 11
Children with ADHD and their families 12
ADHD in Boys... 15
The Most Common Signs and Symptoms of ADHD in Boys.18

Chapter 2 What Schools Can Do..........................21

The school's obligations and role in diagnosing ADHD.......21
Observations to Keep in the Back of Your Mind 22
Caution and Tips for Teachers 24

Chapter 3 Medications for Children and
Teenagers: Guidance for School Personnel and
Parents 25

Educators' Essential Knowledge 25
Educating Parents...29

Chapter 4 Behavior Therapy for Managing
ADHD 33

Treatment of ADHD with Behavior Therapy (Psychosocial
Interventions)..33
The Basics of Behavioral Therapy 35
Behavioral Treatment for the Family at Home 36
Behavioral Support in the Classroom...................... 38
Behavioral Therapy for Children 40

Chapter 5 Guidelines for Managing Attention Deficit Hyperactivity Disorder in Boys 41

1. Use More Immediate Consequences *41*
2. Consequences should be used more frequently. *42*
3. Employing More Salient Consequences *44*
4. Incentives should begin before penalties. *45*
5. Consistency is key. *46*
6. Prepare for Unexpected Obstacles and Shifts in Situations. *47*
7. Keep a Disability Perspective *49*
8. Exercise the Art of Forgiveness. *50*

Chapter 6 Educational Approaches for Boys 53

Here are several effective ways to assist your boy with ADHD to learn: *54*

Chapter 7 12 Effective Discipline Techniques ... 59

Disciplining an ADHD child: A few practical pointers *59*

Chapter 8 Students' Guide to Studying & Doing Homework 67

Chapter 9 Diet for Your ADHD Boy 77

The Importance of a Kid's ADHD Diet *77*
ADHD and nutrients *79*
ADHD, medication, and appetite *79*
ADHD Nutrition for Children *80*
ADHD Diets: Is There a Standardized One? *81*
How Effective is an ADHD-Focused Diet? *82*
What Foods Should Your Child Stay Away From? *85*
The most important nutrients for treating ADHD *87*
How to Feed an ADHD Child *91*
Foods That Can Help Treat or Prevent ADHD *92*

What You Should Know Before Feeding an ADHD Diet to Your Child..*93*

Chapter 10 Strategies to Manage ADHD Behaviors (Part 1) **99**

Chapter 11 Strategies to Manage ADHD Behaviors (Part 2)..**123**

Chapter 12 ADHD in the Schoolyard................**143**

Chapter 13 Tips for Parents on How to Take Care of Themselves..**153**

Tips for parents of children with ADHD on how to care for themselves.. ....*153*
Suggestions for Parents of Children with ADHD Regarding Self-Care...*154*
Affirmations...*157*
Top self-care suggestions for parents of ADHD children ..*159*
The Family Priority Exercise *164*

Conclusion...**167**

Reference...**170**

Introduction

If you have a boy with ADHD, you may have asked, "What is so difficult?" Why does he repeatedly make the same mistakes? What does he lack? You feel as though you are living in the film Groundhog Day, as the same unwanted behaviors persist despite your best efforts. You adore your son, but you are perpetually irritated and, on a deeper level, terrified. You think, "What will become of my son if he can't pull himself together?" Is he destined to spend his entire life working in low-paying, unfulfilling jobs? Parenting a boy at any age is challenging. Parenting a boy with ADHD may sometimes feel like progress peaks are frequently followed by significant regressions. Why do children with ADHD often have a more difficult time with regular tasks? They appear to be challenged academically, socially, and psychologically.

They forget things, are unable to settle down, have trouble concentrating, and zone out regularly. They are disorganized, overburdened, emotionally uncontrolled, and oblivious to the nuances of peer interactions. While they cherish their creativity, "outside-the-box" thinking, and vitality, they are often ashamed of their weaknesses, seek to avoid confronting them, and feel powerless to change them. They, like many other children, want nothing more than to be "normal. "They are adamantly opposed to having a "condition," and regardless of how often you remind them that everyone's brain is different, they believe it is surely more than a "focus issue." How can you feel competent and useful while you assist them in conquering daily challenges and embracing their intelligence? How can you listen to what they have to say about their experiences and provide them with the necessary empathy and direction? These two issues are inextricably linked. It is equally difficult for them as it is for you.

What is exactly ADHD?

Normal childhood behaviors include forgetting assignments, daydreaming in class, and acting impulsively. ADHD is characterized by impulsivity and hyperactivity. Many children are diagnosed with ADHD before the age of seven, which is a common sign of a neurodevelopmental disorder. Children with ADHD may have difficulty controlling their spontaneous actions, such as movement, speech, and focus, all of which can be impaired. Everyone is acquainted with a boy who can not sit still for more than one minute.

They never seem to pay attention, never follow directions, and always say inappropriate things at inappropriate times, despite repeated warnings. It's not very often that these kids are called bad or get in trouble for being lazy or not caring.

It may be challenging to distinguish between "typical child behavior" and ADHD. A diagnosis of ADHD is unlikely if the signs or symptoms are only present in specific situations. Parenting a boy with ADHD can be challenging and stressful, but there are many things you can do to help alleviate symptoms, get through daily problems, and make your family happier.

When they think of ADHD, people see a youngster that is always active, leaping, and disrupting others. However, the situation is somewhat more difficult. Some kids with ADHD are active and interested, while others are lazy and easily bored.

Children can be somewhat lethargic, but they are not always impulsive or hyperactive. Common symptoms of ADHD include impulsivity, inattention, and a propensity for erratic conduct. Children with simple inattention symptoms of ADHD are frequently deemed undiagnosed since they are not disruptive. Distraction can lead to not listening to adults like parents and teachers, doing poorly in school, and even getting into fights with other kids.

We now have a solid understanding of what ADHD is. We have a vast understanding of its effects on the brain. We have never had a better professional viewpoint. And why do the symptoms make day-to-day life seem like a struggle? Best of all, we have medicines that are so effective that, for the first time in their lives, many individuals compete on a level playing field. You will learn about them in the following pages. And based on a theory regarding the nature of ADHD, this book offers a series of strategies that can alter your son's life at home, at school, and with your family and friends. These strategies are founded on a scientific understanding of the mechanics underlying ADHD symptoms, and they can help your boy succeed in all the areas that matter.

Parenting any child is a challenging endeavor. However, parenting an ADHD boy might feel like a succession of progress peaks followed by sharp regressions. Why is life often more challenging for ADHD children? They appear to have cognitive, social, and psychological issues. They frequently forget things, cannot slow down, have trouble concentrating, and have difficulty concentrating and focusing. They are disorganized, overwhelmed, emotionally uncontrolled, and oblivious to the nuances of peer interactions. While they value their creativity, "outside the box" thinking, and enthusiasm, they are often ashamed of their weaknesses, seek to avoid dealing with them, and feel powerless to change them.

Through the perspectives of children and adolescents with ADHD, this book intends to help you become a competent parent. You will encourage and listen to your son's ADHD-related stories, and you will answer with understanding, support, and calmness. You will understand what your son is communicating to you through his words and actions. You will work together to overcome common difficulties. Your son will come to consider you a buddy. If people feel heard and observed, they will be more receptive to your remarks. You will experience less stress, and your son's development will improve.

My years of experience working with children diagnosed with AHDH qualify me to devise the most efficient methods for enhancing their social and behavioral skills. Children with ADHD are able to excel academically and maintain self-control at home. This is why I wrote this book: to aid individuals in recognizing their potential. As an expert in the field of rehabilitation, I can confidently state that nothing is impossible for a youngster with ADHD. They require the simple trust of their parents and the community. Parents of children with ADHD must demonstrate extraordinary patience and concentration. Parents must demonstrate a strong, consistent, and dependable commitment to the well-being of their children. This is very important for a child with ADHD who lives in a society that doesn't understand their specific goals and needs.

There is hope.

Despite everything, I hope that this book brings you hope. I hope your family has options to choose from. I hope this is not the greatest it will ever be. I wish nothing but the best for you, your family, and your ADHD son in the future. This book contains efficient natural therapies to alleviate your son's symptoms of ADHD.

I have no doubt that you did not pick up this book by accident, given that natural therapies are effective. Perhaps you purchased it because you wanted to try a natural solution before resorting to medication for your son. Perhaps you turned to it after failing to find relief with medication. Whatever led you to this book was not a plain chance. You are here because you require assistance, and I hope that this book properly meets your needs. Many years ago, I walked alone along this path with my son. No parent should face this challenge alone. Realize that you are not alone when things become challenging. You've got this, and I got you!

Before we get started, I would like to express my gratitude. I'm certain this is not the first book you've encountered, but you chose to read it nonetheless. You may have selected from a choice of courses and manuals that promise to make you an ideal and well-rounded parent while you grow your ADHD children to their full potential. Nevertheless, for whatever reason, mine stuck out, and this currently makes me the happiest person on the planet. I tell you that this will be a worthwhile read if you endure. In the following pages, you will discover the most effective techniques to raise your ADHD boy so that he develops into the best version of himself. Additionally, you will learn a great deal about what it takes to be a good parent.

A number of simple-to-effective tactics for treating ADHD in boys, as well as nonprescription alternatives, will be reviewed in depth. You will learn about the family-wide benefits of counseling. You will now have the opportunity to discover practical ways of living with an ADHD child and regulating their behaviors at home. There are also suggestions for discipline and ideas for activities to keep your boy occupied. Upon completion of your ADHD education, you will discover a fantastic approach for discovering the positive aspects of ADHD and how your son can live a completely normal life. ADHD is not the end of your son's story; it is simply the beginning of the next chapter! Every attempt was made to ensure that this guide contained the maximum amount of valuable information. Please enjoy!

Chapter 1
Understanding ADHD

Attention deficit hyperactivity disorder (ADHD) is most common in children and is characterized by not being able to focus, acting on impulse, and, in some cases, being overly active. In most cases, both of these signs and symptoms coexist, but it is possible for one to appear without the other. By the time a child reaches the age of seven, he is likely to be showing signs of hyperactivity. A child's inability to focus or pay attention may not be apparent until he enters the rigorous world of primary school. As many as 5% to 11% of American children are affected by ADHD, which is one of the most frequent childhood conditions. When kids have ADHD, they might be impulsive, fidgety, have trouble focusing, talking too much, having trouble following directions, being hyperactive, or having trouble waiting their turn.

Are there any typical symptoms?

Your little one is a wiggle worm. He is unable to sit still and continuously fidgets. Because of this, he frequently misses deadlines and barely completes half of the tasks he's given. Your kid frequently interrupts the class by yelling out replies, deviating off subject, or standing up from his seat. Medical professionals are the only ones qualified to diagnose and treat children with ADHD. Parents and teachers need to be aware of the warning signs of ADHD in order to help a child get the help and accommodations they need.

What is the difference between the many types of attention deficit hyperactivity disorder?

The most common kinds of ADHD

The following are the three most common kinds of ADHD:

- Inattentive Type ADHD
  A lack of focus and distractibility are the hallmarks of inattentive type ADHD.

- Hyperactive-Impulsive Type ADHD
  This kind of ADHD is marked by being hyperactive and acting on impulses, but there are no signs of not paying attention.

- Combined Type ADHD
  A combination of inattentive-distracted and hyperactive-impulsive behavior is the hallmark of Combined Type ADHD.

Inattention

- The short attention span
- The inability to pay attention to details and being easily distracted.

- Poor organizational skills
- Poor study skills

Impulsivity

- Interrupts people frequently.
- Has a hard time waiting for one's turn in school or social circumstances.
- Tends to blurt out replies rather than wait to be prompted.
- Prone to taking risks and acting rashly.

Hyperactivity

- Constantly running or climbing. Appears to have no clear goal other than to keep moving.
- Has difficulty remaining seated even when instructed to do so.
- Wriggling in his seat or fidgeting with his hands excessively, excessive fidgeting
- Inability to focus; switching between tasks without completing any
- Struggles to engage in peaceful activities
- Loses or forgets things frequently

Risk factors

The following variables may increase your boy's risk of developing ADHD:

- Family members with ADHD or a mental illness, such as parents or siblings

- Increased exposure to dangerous chemicals like lead, which is often found in the paint and pipes of older buildings.
- Pregnant women who use drugs drink alcohol or smoke
- Premature birth

Children with ADHD and their families

Because ADHD affects the entire family, it is crucial to be aware of the difficulties that arise when one or more of the children suffers from the illness. These families' difficulties are frequently overlooked or ignored by educators and others. For the following reasons, families with individuals who have ADHD are under a lot more stress than ordinary families:

- Homework, getting ready for school, and bedtime all provide significant challenges.
- Parents often disagree with each other about how to treat, discipline, manage, structure, and other parts of their children's lives.
- If one or both parents blame each other for their child's difficulties, it can be difficult for the child to get the help they need. Because of this conflict, marital stress is severe, and divorce and separation rates are higher than they are in the general population.

- With so much to deal with on a daily basis, it can be physically and emotionally draining for the mother.
- Many parents find that having to constantly watch or take care of their toddlers takes up a lot of time and makes it hard to do things like housework and other chores.
- It can be quite stressful for parents to deal with a child with ADHD who is also extremely stubborn, belligerent, and angry.
- Parents of children with ADHD must continuously justify both their parenting choices and their child's condition. In order to provide their children with the appropriate interventions and treatments, they must listen to the negative publicity about this condition and resist common opinions.
- Families, friends, and acquaintances may provide criticism and suggestions about how parents should discipline and parent their children. Because of the stress they face every day, parents' confidence in their parenting abilities is shaken to the core.
- The exclusion of a child from out-of-school activities is a common problem for families. When your child is left out of birthday celebrations or struggles to make and keep friends, it can be heartbreaking.

- Because of their sibling's ADHD, siblings can be resentful or even jealous of the time and attention this child receives in the family schedule, routines, and activities. A terrible reputation for one's brother or sister can have a devastating effect on one's siblings, who feel wounded and embarrassed.
- Parents whose kids have ADHD may feel alone and not get enough help from their extended families.
- Parents are expected to take a more active role in their child's education, and well-being than the majority of parents do. Parents must also learn about ADHD, research-validated therapies, their child's educational rights under the law, and other things to be effective advocates for their child's needs.

Consider these points when making your decisions.

- More than one person in the family (a parent or a sibling) is prone to suffering from ADHD.
- Other members of the family who suffer from ADHD are frequently undiagnosed, leaving them to survive on their own without the assistance and care they need. Because of this, the professionals who specialize in treating children with ADHD stress the importance of looking at treatment in the context of the family, which is why they feel it is crucial.

Developing an effective treatment plan for a child requires knowledge of the child's family (such as how the members communicate and how they enforce discipline).

- Many parents realize after their child is diagnosed with ADHD that they have been dealing with their own undiagnosed ADHD for years. This new information could change the way the family works for the better.
- Support and understanding are critical for the families of children with ADHD. The good news for parents is that there is a wide range of resources available to them.

ADHD in Boys

Hyperactivity is the only symptom of ADHD. It's a trait that only boys have. Boys are more likely than girls to be diagnosed with ADHD, despite the fact that the disorder affects both sexes equally. As a result, boys are more likely to exhibit symptoms of hyperactivity than girls. Hyperactivity, in particular, may be easier to detect than other signs of ADHD. Boys with ADHD are sometimes picked on or told off for being too impulsive and active in their everyday lives.

They may have a lot of problems at school and at home. It's also possible that their actions can alienate other children, making it difficult to make friends. ADHD is a condition that affects a boy in a unique way. Other

ADHD issues, such as difficulty focusing, are common in boys with ADHD. In many circumstances, boys' experiences with ADHD might differ greatly from those of girls.

What do boys with ADHD look like?

The boy's hyperactive behavior is difficult to miss. You might see this:

- Even when playing indoors, boys run around and yell.
- Playing too hard could
- Buffering up against people and objects
- Even when seated, they are constantly moving.

This type of conduct is more likely to raise red flags at home and in school than other indicators of ADHD, such as difficulty concentrating. As a result, children diagnosed with ADHD are more likely to be boys than girls. However, not all guys with ADHD are impulsive. Other common signs of ADHD include hyperactivity and impulsivity.

ADHD behavior and "being bad."

Attention-seeking boys with ADHD are more likely to stand out. A positive or negative outcome can result from this. A benefit is that they are more likely to be diagnosed and treated for their ADHD early on. Teachers, siblings, coaches, and other families may give them a lot of negative comments. As a result, boys' self-esteem may suffer, and they may become more disruptive, which may lead to behavioral issues.

Boys who suffer from excessive energy may have a difficult time adjusting to adult life. Those with ADHD who aren't hyperactive should be aware of this. That, too, may have repercussions. Boys who aren't hyperactive are more likely to be overlooked since they don't fit the stereotype (much like girls are). They may be spared the ill will, but they may also be denied the assistance they require.

Making friends is difficult for those with ADHD.

Making and keeping friends is a common problem for children with ADHD. Boys, on the other hand, confront a distinct set of social difficulties. Often, they are supposed to be tough and flexible. However, many children with ADHD struggle with emotional regulation. In addition, they aren't always accurate in their interpretations of social cues and cue sequences. For their own sake and that of their peers, boys with ADHD may act like the class clown in order to hide their difficulties. However, this kind of behavior might backfire. While their antics can be amusing, some children may find them obtrusive. The greatest way to help your child comprehend social issues is to talk honestly about them with him.

The Most Common Signs and Symptoms of ADHD in Boys

In boys, hyperactivity and impulsivity are not the hallmarks of ADHD. ADHD symptoms like not being able to see things from other people's points of view, getting upset easily when rejected, and not being able to remember what happened in the past are more common in teens.

1. **Problems with Self-Directed Communication**

   We all conduct a private conversation with ourselves in our heads. ADHD sufferers don't always hear their own "brain coach" or internal dialogue. In the case of ADHD, your brain coach's volume is set too low. Self-directed dialogue is present, but it's not getting through.

2. **Hyper-focusing on Things**

   The most common question parents ask is, "How can I improve my son's focus?" Experts discovered that medication and working with children to help them build their own self-directed discourse are solutions that experts discovered, and even then, it takes a long time. Focusing a lot on what your son is interested in could help him be successful in his career and in life.

3. **A lack of recollection**

Those with ADHD have a hard time recalling their past events and the feelings they evoked. If your boy tells you he can't remember how to do anything you've taught him, that may be the case.

4. **Inability to Plan for the Future**

Those with ADHD have a hard time envisioning the future since they tend to live in the now. There is a reason why a promise of a prize on Friday night didn't work for your son if they completed their homework every day this week: the reward is too far away.

5. **It's difficult to tell how much time has passed.**

Boys with ADHD have a hard time grasping the sense of time as something tangible. It's common for them to argue about a task for longer than it takes to do it since they can't see how much time is required.

6. **Inability to See Things from a Different Angle**

Reading social cues indicates that your son has a problem with perspective-taking—the ability to comprehend other people's ideas and feelings while also being aware of his own behavior. If your son doesn't have the ability to see things from another person's point of view, he doesn't have empathy.

7. **Having a Hard Time Putting the Amount of the Problem into Perspective**

   Boys with ADHD may either overreact or underreact to a situation because of their condition.

8. **Impatience in the Face of Sudden Change**

   When they have to do things like stop playing video games and start doing schoolwork, it's difficult since they don't have time to prepare for the transition from the desired task to a less preferred task.

9. **Dysphoria Associated with Sensitivity to Rejection**

   As a result of their condition, boys with ADHD are more sensitive to perceived or actual rejection. Boys with ADHD have a strong reaction to rejection and tend to live in large emotional states. Recognition Response Euphoria is the reverse of this. When praise and acknowledgment are given with the intention of helping a boy see their own abilities, those with ADHD are more receptive to it than those without it. Recognize your son's efforts when he does something well.

Chapter 2
What Schools Can Do

The school's obligations and role in diagnosing ADHD

Details regarding the ongoing activities at the school

- The boy will spend a significant portion of his life at school, making it an important environment.

- The boy's teacher is in the best position to report on how well the boy is doing in school in comparison to other students of the same age and grade. No one else is in a better position. This comprises the teacher's observations and statistics regarding the boy's performance in school as well as how well he is doing socially, emotionally, and behaviorally. Also included are the teacher's thoughts and feelings about the boy.

- The teacher must be prepared to discuss the boy's capacity to remain in control, stay on target, engage with classmates and adults, start and finish assignments, and do a range of other things.

- As part of proper screening for ADHD, teachers will be asked to describe what they have noticed about the student.
- Work samples and disciplinary referrals, which can be found in the records of guidance counselors or administrators, are two more things that may be helpful to know about a student's current academic and behavioral performance at school.
- Observation of the student's classroom performance as well as in other settings such as the playground or the cafeteria provides useful evidence of potential issues the boy may be exhibiting with regard to work production, social interactions, disruptive or off-task behavior, and disorganization in comparison to other students. It is obviously more useful for evaluators to obtain observational data from the school rather than simply view the boy in the unnatural environment of a doctor's office.

Observations to Keep in the Back of Your Mind

- Evaluators must also establish whether the symptoms are causing the student difficulties and interfering with his functioning (for example, in social and interpersonal connections, academic productivity, or disruptive behavioral issues) and to what extent. Children's everyday interactions with and observations of teachers and other school workers make them the most qualified sources of this data.

- In the diagnostic process, parents have a right to anticipate that the school will be supportive and responsive. Doctors and mental health professionals doing clinical evaluations for ADHD need schools to give them the information they need.

- Parents must sign a release-of-information form for the school to talk to experts outside of the school or give documents and information about the boy.

- For evaluations like behavioral rating scales, school employees should be timely and thorough in giving the needed information.

- The teacher's thoughts on the boy's behavior, social skills, work output, and so on can also be beneficial (and may be requested) if a paragraph or two is written by the teacher.

- To make the most of a physician's limited time, it is highly advised that schools deliver information in a format that is easy to read and understand. One to two pages of information about the boy's educational history and current performance is ideal.

Caution and Tips for Teachers

- It is crucial that school staff are careful how they explain to parents their concerns that a kid might have ADHD since there are liabilities that may be incurred if it is not stated properly. For example, school districts may not want teachers to alert parents that their child has to undergo a medical evaluation since the district may be required to pay for it. Many children with ADHD are diagnosed and treated successfully thanks to the intervention of an attentive and supportive teacher. Teachers have a duty to inform parents.

- Discussing the potential that a child's difficulties could be caused by an underlying medical condition or disorder is usually best done in a group setting with parents. At a minimum, one additional school professional—the school nurse, guidance counselor, administrator, or school psychologist, should accompany the classroom teacher in doing so.

Chapter 3
Medications for Children and Teenagers: Guidance for School Personnel and Parents

Educators' Essential Knowledge

- The decision to put their child on medicine is not one that is taken lightly by parents They are concerned about the long-term implications of their actions. Well-meaning family members, friends, and acquaintances who don't know about effective treatments or who are against using drugs because of bad information often make them feel terrible.

- The school's job is to provide full support and cooperation for any student undergoing pharmaceutical treatment. So that the doctor can monitor the child's response to the medication, school personnel must share their observations. When starting a new drug, it's critical to keep an eye on the patient's progress and report back to the doctor as often as possible.

- A teacher must be able to keep track of a boy's academic, social, and behavioral progress while he is being treated for his condition with psychotropic medication. When students are taking medicine, teachers must keep a close eye on them and report any changes they notice.

- Production of goods and services (starting on and completing assignments).
- Maintaining focus and staying on task
- Listening attentively and obeying orders
- Consciousness and vigilance
- Insomnia and a high degree of activity
- Self-control and impulsiveness
- Relationships between people

- It doesn't matter how long a student has been on medication for ADHD; they need to be checked out during school hours. This is essential in order to get the full benefit of the drug for the child or adolescent.

- During the titration phase, they should be prepared to offer their feedback on the student's performance.

- Teachers' evaluation forms can be sent straight from the doctor's office, or parents can give them to the school in person.

- In most cases, the school nurse serves as the go-between for parents and teachers when it comes to properly administering medication in the classroom. For the best results, it is critical that all parties involved work together in harmony and communicate openly.

- Medications, doses, and times of administration are frequently tinkered with until the optimal combination is established for the patient. It's crucial to keep in touch with parents and alert them to any changes in their child's conduct. Some parents wait to hear if the teacher observes a difference before disclosing to the school that their child has begun taking medicine (or that their child's prescription or dosage has changed).

- Medication is metabolized at a different rate in children. Keep an eye out for any shifts in behavior or issues that crop up throughout the day to make sure the drug is working properly (for example, in the afternoon).

- Teachers should notify parents (and the school nurse, if one is available) of any side effects they are concerned about. There should be no change in personality or the appearance of sedation or lethargy in children receiving ADHD drugs. If this is the case, the youngster may be taking too much medication, or a different type of medication is required.

- For this reason, students with ADHD who are taking stimulant drugs may not be eating enough at breakfast or lunch. They may be hungry at various points during the day and would benefit from being given a snack if necessary.

- Students continue to use these fast-acting stimulant drugs. For students who must take a dose during school hours, it is critical that the medication be administered exactly when the doctor instructs them to do so.

- Rebound effects may occur in certain children after medicine wears off. Children may be discovered screaming, fighting, or getting into difficulty in the playground or cafeteria if their next scheduled dose is not given on time. The second dose of medication takes effect after around thirty minutes. Avoiding the "rebound effect" by planning ahead of time is quite beneficial.

- As a result of their ADHD and executive function impairment, students with ADHD have a difficult time remembering to go to the office at the designated time to take their prescribed medicine. Teachers and other school personnel have the duty to gently remind students. This can be done in a number of ways, such as with a beeper watch or a vibrating alarm, or with private teacher signals, timed coded spoken reminders, or a sticker chart at the pharmacy where the prescription is filled.

- Before the school's medication supply runs out, parents should be notified, so they have time to renew the prescription and bring it to school.

Educating Parents

- Children who are taking medicine should be monitored by their parents to ensure that they receive their doses on time and consistently.
- It is critical that the drug be closely monitored and managed. If it is given in different ways, the child would be better off without it.
- Seeking medical advice is the most effective way to deal with appetite suppression, such as scheduling breakfast and other meals at times when your child is more likely to be hungry, as this is a common side effect.
- Because the school is not involved in providing a noon dose of a long-acting medication, some parents may be tempted to keep their child's medication for ADHD a secret. This should not be done. Medical therapy for a mental illness should not be kept secret from the teacher.
- For a child to get the most out of medication treatment, a team effort and close communication between the home, school, and physician are needed. Parents should be in charge of this communication so that the doctor gets the important information from the school

about how their child is doing while taking medicine.

- Monitoring the medication's effectiveness necessitates regular follow-up appointments with the child's doctor.

- When your child is taking medicine, you and the school must be involved in the doctor's care.

- The doctor will always conduct a trial period before prescribing medication to a child in order to find the most beneficial combination of drug and dosage. They have the good fortune of promptly receiving treatment that has a considerable impact on their symptoms. The medication may not work for everyone, and some people may not be able to use it at all. Medication is said to help 70 to 90 percent of ADHD children. Parents must be patient and understand that this procedure may take some time to perfect. Chances are if one of the prescriptions fails to help, another one will.

- There are tight regulations in place for the prescription and dispensing of routinely prescribed stimulants since they are designated by the DEA as Schedule II drugs. Pharmacists are regulated by the Food and Drug Administration (FDA). Refilling medications will be more difficult as a result of this. Because the drug cannot be called in or prescribed for more than one month, it is not possible to get refills.

- If a doctor gives a child a short-acting stimulant, parents should keep a close eye on them and talk to the school nurse to make sure the drug is there.

- It is important for children to understand why they are taking their medication and how it affects them. Those taking medication should be aware that they are in control of their actions, but the medication helps them (pay attention, get school and homework done, put on the brakes so they can make better choices, and so forth). It is possible to provide children with a variety of tools to help them better understand ADHD and the reasons they are prescribed medication to manage it.

- When it comes to ADHD therapy, parents need to be aware of both medication and other multimodal strategies that have been shown to be beneficial. Parents who have concerns about their child's medicine should speak with their doctor and make sure they have all the information they require, as well as consult other trustworthy sources.

Chapter 4
Behavior Therapy for Managing ADHD

Treatment of ADHD with Behavior Therapy (Psychosocial Interventions)

- Two research-validated therapies have been shown to be particularly successful in the management of ADHD: behavior therapy and cognitive behavioral therapy. For some children, medication is all that is needed to alleviate their symptoms of ADHD and other behavioral issues. Many children with ADHD benefit most from a combination of behavioral therapy and pharmaceutical therapy, which can have a significant impact on their functioning, behavior, and relationships. Behavior therapy is a must-have for any child with ADHD who is not on medication.

- For children aged four to five, behavioral therapy should be used as the first line of treatment; for children aged six to eleven, doctors should recommend FDA-approved medication or evidence-based treatment for ADHD provided by parents and teachers.

- Parent and teacher education in behavior modification techniques is essential in behavior therapy, as is the adult's dedication to putting the ideas into practice. It's not an easy task, but the rewards are well worth the effort.
- Children's behavior can be improved by teaching adults how to use behavioral concepts and tactics to control their children's misbehavior.
- Behavioral therapy helps children and their families by teaching them new ways of dealing with difficulties and connecting with others. Changing the way adults respond to the child's or teen's behavior teaches the youngster or teenager new ways of acting.

Treatments for ADHD may include the following: Behavioral and psychological therapies

- Involved parents and well-managed classrooms are key to a successful home and school environment.
- Behavior management approaches used by parents and teachers have been proven to be beneficial.
- Complimentary communication, which means enabling a youngster to listen to and follow instructions from their parents or teachers

- Be aware of the antecedents or triggers that lead to misbehavior in order to avert difficulties at home and in the school environment.
- Developing coping mechanisms for dealing with ADHD's problematic behaviors at school and at home
- Programs and services for social and emotional learning in the classroom and throughout the school
- Enhancing a child's ability to interact socially with their peers
- Behavior programs can be set up, such as daily charts and report cards from school to home, token economy programs, and personalized behavior contracts.

The Basics of Behavioral Therapy

- Behavioral intervention for ADHD relies heavily on the use of behavior modification strategies.
- Based on the A–B–Cs of behavior: antecedent–behavior–concomitant. To put it simply, an antecedent (A) is something that sets off a behavior (B). The immediate result (C) is what happens as a direct result of the demonstrated behavior (B). Because of the outcomes, the likelihood that the behavior will occur again will either increase or decrease.

- In order to lessen or eliminate behavioral problems, it is important to learn how to identify and change the antecedents or triggers that cause them in the first place.
- Incentive systems (such as points or token systems) are used in behavior control techniques. The use of rewards can help to improve behavior.
- When used effectively and wisely, negative consequences or punishments, like time-outs and the loss of privileges, are just as important and useful for changing behavior.

Behavioral Treatment for the Family at Home

- Behavioral management ideas and approaches for children with ADHD are significantly more complex than those for ordinary children. They must be taught how to deal with the daily struggles and behavioral issues that come with caring for a child who has a condition.
- It is imperative that parents receive education about their children's disorders in order to provide the best care possible. Parent training programs use a variety of methods to improve interactions between parents and children, reduce noncompliance, reduce behavioral

problems, and make it easier for families to talk to each other.

- Parents are taught how to use rewards and punishments in a way that is both effective and preventative.
- Parent education can be delivered in a classroom setting or one-on-one with a small group of parents over the course of several weeks.
- As a general rule, parents of preschool and elementary-school-aged children benefit from behavior modification training. Other tactics and abilities, such as behavioral contracting and problem-solving, are taught to parents and teens as they get older.
- When parents go to a program to learn how to be better parents, they are given homework to do between sessions.
- Parenting classes typically cover topics like creating daily routines, organizing and structuring the home for success, rewarding appropriate behavior, giving clear instructions and commands that increase compliance and cooperation, avoiding power struggles and conflicts, and utilizing incentive systems such as daily charts, point, and token systems, and school-home note systems. These are just a few of the more common topics covered.

- Parents must also be aware of how behavioral principles affect their own behavior if they hope to have any effect on their child's behavior. Parental frustration can lead to sanctions that actually exacerbate rather than diminish a child's misbehavior.

Behavioral Support in the Classroom

School-based behavioral interventions have been demonstrated to be successful in reducing children's bad conduct. Most school-based behavior interventions are done by teachers, and they usually involve the following steps:

- Active management of the classroom
- Creating an ADHD-friendly learning environment in a classroom.
- Transitions and other stressful times during the school day can make it easier for students to act up.
- Implementing mechanisms to monitor student conduct in the classroom.
- Implementing tailored behavioral programs, supports, and interventions, such as daily report cards and behavior contracts,
- Adopting specific measures to assist students who display symptoms of inattention, distraction, impulsivity, or hyperactivity controls

kids' negative feelings, such as rage and impatience, and improves their self-regulation.

- With a systematic and coordinated whole-school effort, school districts across the United States are moving their focus from reacting to negative behavior to fostering positive behavior. As part of this process, teachers should model and teach in all classes and school-wide the rules and expected behaviors, as well as provide a safe and supportive atmosphere for all children.

- In many schools nowadays, there is a multi-tiered support system for students (MTSS), which is a progression of ever-increasing support. Both RTI and PBIS are MTSS models that work well for helping students who need it with their behavior in an educational setting.

- As an example, in PBIS schools, students are taught and rewarded for doing good things as a tier 1 intervention. More specific and intensive support (tiers 2 and 3) are provided to students who require them, and their responses to the interventions are closely monitored to ensure that all students receive the assistance they require.

Behavioral Therapy for Children

- Peer relationships are the focus of child-centered therapy. They are most common in classrooms, small groups at school, in office clinics, and in summer camps.
- Coaching, modeling, role-playing, feedback, rewards, and consequences are all part of child-based treatments. Practicing skills taught in natural settings where the kid is engaged with peers is a key component of all of these programs.
- Prosocial skills and behaviors are taught, practiced, and reinforced via research-validated child-based treatments.

Chapter 5
Guidelines for Managing Attention Deficit Hyperactivity Disorder in Boys

Given that boys with ADHD are less sensitive to behavioral consequences like rewards and penalties, current thinking suggests that particular behavioral management recommendations should be applied to these boys. These approaches have been shown to be quite helpful in building both home and school management plans for children with ADHD. If you are a practitioner or educator who advises parents on how to manage their child's ADHD, you should constantly keep these things in mind. If you stick to these eight guidelines while creating management programs, you won't go far wrong:

1. Use More Immediate Consequences

ADHD children need more immediate feedback or sanctions for their behavior and activities than other children. ADHD affects how often youngsters receive feedback on whether or not their behavior is socially acceptable. Depending on their age, it's possible that praising typical young people merely a few times a day is sufficient. It was discovered many years ago by experts like Virginia Douglas and others that children with ADHD are more susceptible to being impacted by sudden consequences or shifts in their environment. According to research, ADHD children appear less rule-governed and more contingency-shaped in daily situations in comparison to their typically developing classmates.

This is especially true when parents are trying to change their children's undesirable behaviors into more productive ones. Children with ADHD learn most from corrections that are clear, direct, and given as soon as possible after the behavior is corrected. Praise and feedback are acceptable forms of feedback, but they should be specific about what the child did that was perceived as a positive action. Additional privileges or even a food treat might be used as a means of showing affection. The ADHD child's behavior must be changed more quickly. It doesn't matter what kind of feedback is given to ADHD youngsters; the faster the response time, the better.

2. Consequences should be used more frequently.

Children with ADHD are more likely to be punished for their bad behavior. Children's caregivers must respond more frequently than typical children's caregivers in letting them know how they are progressing. It's true that if this is done too frequently, it might irritate and interfere with the daily activities of children with ADHD. Parents may find this tiresome, but they should be urged to increase the frequency of feedback and consequences for their children with ADHD. Place little stickers with smiling faces around the house in places where the children frequently glance each day in order to encourage them to be more positive. Bathroom mirrors, clocks, the inside of refrigerators, bread boxes, and the back and front doors are all examples of places where this can be found. Every time a caregiver sees a sticker, they are supposed to say something positive about their child's ADHD. Alternatively, a cooking timer could be set for short and different periods throughout the day by parents or teachers in order to achieve this purpose. When it goes off, it serves as a gentle reminder to parents to go out and check on their ADHD children. To reward children for good behavior, it is necessary to praise them and even award them for good behavior.

A reprimand or a light penalty may be required if regulations are broken. Another tool for teaching parents to provide frequent feedback is the MotivAider. Take, for example, this tiny vibrating box with an integrated digital timer, which can be set to go off every 20 minutes. The compact device is carried by the caregiver in the form of a belt loop or a pocket. When it vibrates, it is a signal to parents that their ADHD youngster needs input. An additional benefit of this strategy is that it is less clear to children that they are being rewarded by their parents or teachers, so the praise they get may appear more genuine to them.

3. Employing More Salient Consequences

In order to get a child with ADHD to do their homework, follow the rules, or behave properly, they need more obvious or powerful consequences than children without ADHD do. Using larger, more important, or more obvious incentives may be necessary for children with ADHD because their reward and consequence sensitivity may be diminished. Furthermore, verbal praise or compliments are rarely enough to motivate youngsters (ADHD). Additional rewards, such as physical affection, special treats, tokens or points, and small toys or collectibles, may be necessary to encourage ADHD children to work or adhere to important rules in addition to verbal praise.

This is especially true for children who have difficulty focusing in school or at home. Even though it appears to go against the conventional idea that children shouldn't receive cash rewards too frequently, this may actually be a good thing for them because it keeps them motivated to keep doing what they're already doing. The fulfillment that comes from pleasing one's loved ones;

the accomplishment of mastering a new talent; or the admiration of one's peers for a job well done are examples of intrinsic joys. Because children with ADHD do not respond as well to rewards as a form of reinforcement, they are less likely to be motivated in the same way by different types of rewards. Because of how ADHD works, children with it may need more serious and sometimes even material consequences at first to help them learn and keep good habits.

4. Incentives should begin before penalties.

You must retain an open mind in order to prevent the all-too-common tendency toward punishing people in order to curb bad conduct. Caretakers must be frequently reminded of the rules that indicate "positives come before negatives" when implementing behavior-change programs. A caregiver who wishes to alter an ADHD child's undesirable or poor behavior must first transform the issue behavior into a desirable or good alternative. Observing and rewarding positive behavior will automatically follow. After at least a week of continuously praising this new behavior, parents or instructors should criticize the opposing conduct. However, parents must be reminded to impose discipline only when the child demonstrates specific, negative conduct in question and not for everything the child may be doing incorrectly. When used with mild punishment, an incentive program, and a ratio of one punishment for every two or three times someone is praised or given a reward, it can be effective at changing behavior.

5. Consistency is key.

The guidelines cannot simply be stated to caretakers; rather, the terms must be defined. Consistency is defined by three factors. Caregiver consistency is essential. In other words, the way they respond to behaviors they're working on changing in the present is how they should respond to them in the future. Behavior change programs for children with ADHD are doomed to failure because of their inconsistency, unpredictability, and capriciousness in this area. When you're just beginning a behavior-change program, it's crucial not to give up too early. An ADHD child's behavior has taken months or even years to fall into this pattern. It's not going to happen overnight, as common sense implies. Don't get discouraged if a new management strategy doesn't yield immediate or spectacular results. It can take time for behavior modification to have a therapeutic effect, much like medication.

Don't give up on your behavioral modification program until you've tried it for a few weeks. Second, to be consistent implies acting in the same way no matter where or when you are. If a parent has an ADHD child, it is common for that parent to act one way at home and another in public places like markets and restaurants or in the homes of others. This is something you should try to avoid at all costs. If feasible, children with ADHD should be taught that the rules and punishments they are familiar with at home will be enforced when they are away from home. Parents should strive to govern their children's behavior in ways that are as comparable to one another as possible in order to maintain consistency. There will always be differences in parenting styles between fathers and mothers. If one parent punishes an ADHD child while the other ignores or even praises the occurrence of a specific act of misconduct, this is not a good scenario to be in.

6. Prepare for Unexpected Obstacles and Shifts in Situations.

Parents of children with ADHD, especially those who are also defiant, are sometimes confronted with challenging, disruptive, or non-compliant conduct. As well as in one's own home, these kinds of circumstances might occur regularly outside the four walls of one's own home in a variety of public venues. Caregivers may become overwhelmed, befuddled, and frustrated when these situations arise, and they may be unable to come up with rapid solutions. When children with behavior problems act out in public, especially in front of strangers, they are often embarrassed and scared.

When interviewing caregivers of children with ADHD, experts have been struck by their ability to foresee where their children will be disruptive and misbehave if they are pressed to do so. This information has been widely disseminated, but many individuals have failed to put it to good use in anticipating such disasters in the future. This is why experts advise parents to anticipate challenges, think about how to handle them, create a plan, discuss it with their child beforehand, and then use the plan should a problem occur. Many people may find it hard to understand that simply telling a child about the strategy before they enter a dangerous situation dramatically minimizes the likelihood of them engaging in dangerous conduct. But it does, in spite of that fact. Caregivers can make it easier to take care of kids with ADHD by taking four simple steps before going into a tough situation.

- When a possible trouble situation is about to occur, it is best to come to an immediate stop.
- Request that the child repeat two or three simple rules that the child frequently fails to follow in that situation. Children with ADHD and their parents might find it helpful to follow the instructions. "Stand near, don't touch, and don't beg."

- The child should be reminded of the benefits of following the rules and behaving nicely. Incentives like extra playtime or TV time, as well as the option to buy a little present or toy at the end of a trip to the store, can be given to children as a thank you for their cooperation.
- Talk to the youngster about possible punishments. There may be a loss of points or fines, a reduction in privileges for the rest of the day, or even a time out, depending on the severity of the issue. As I've already talked about, the most important part of managing a child well is how quickly a consequence is given in response to a problem.

Once the caregiver and child have gone through these four stages, they may be in a situation that could be troublesome. At this point, the caregiver should start giving the child frequent feedback and small rewards or tokens for good behavior right away.

7. Keep a Disability Perspective

When dealing with an ADHD child who is challenging, caregivers can become outraged, ashamed, or at the very least upset when they are unable to get things to work. It's not uncommon for them to quarrel with the youngster over the matter, just like another child or sibling might. Disappointingly, it may even encourage the child to engage in similar behavior in the future.

Make it clear to caregivers that they are this child's teacher and coach at all times. In order for one of them to remain rational, the parent must step forward. If they lose their cool, it will just make the situation worse, and they'll feel a lot of remorse when they get their bearings back. In order to keep their distance from the child's disruptive behavior, they must pretend to be an outsider who has just come upon this contact between the caregiver and the youngster with ADHD. While this disagreement or interaction is important, it should not be the sole source of one's sense of self-worth and dignity. The best advice you can give them is to be as cool as possible when dealing with their child and to keep a sense of humor about the situation. Caregivers may even need to take a break from the contact for a moment to collect their thoughts and regain control of their emotions. Above all, they should avoid making the child's condition their own. When giving advice to them, remember that they are dealing with a disabled child! Children with ADHD can't control how they act, but their caretakers can step in if they need to.

8. Exercise the Art of Forgiveness.

While this is the most critical rule to follow, it can also be the most challenging. Every night, parents should take a moment to reflect on the day and forgive their children for any mistakes they made during the day. Allow yourself to let go of any negative emotions sparked by your children's misbehavior or disturbances for the day, such as rage, resentment, disappointment, etc. Let them off the hook because they have a disability and can't always control their own actions. This is a critical point to remember. There is no reason why children cannot be taught the importance of taking responsibility for their actions and making amends to those they have harmed. Teachers can do this at the end of the school day when the students have gone home. Breathe in and exhale; let go of the conflicts you have with children who have ADHD during the day.

After forgiving those who may have misunderstood their kids' inappropriate behavior, acted in a way that was offensive to them and their children, or simply dismissed their children as lazy, parents should focus on forgiving themselves and their children for the day's failures. Many of these people don't understand the true nature of ADHD, and as a result, they blame the ADHD child's parents and family for his or her problems when this is plainly not the case. In no way does this imply that parents should continue allowing others to mistreat or misinterpret their child s ADHD condition. In order to prevent this from happening again, it is vital to take corrective action and advocate for these children. As a result of these experiences, it is necessary for parents to develop the ability to look past their own feelings of disappointment, rage, and bitterness.

Teachers may not need to take these precautions because they have a lower emotional attachment to ADHD children than parents do. In spite of this, teachers who are truly empathic may feel guilty if other teachers make fun of them for their management issues with ADHD students. This aspect of forgiveness may be particularly difficult for such educators to master. As a last step, caregivers need to practice forgiving themselves for the mistakes they made in the care of children with ADHD on that specific day. Children with ADHD are known to bring out the worst in adults, which often leads to adults feeling terrible about their own mistakes in dealing with the children. In no way should parents or instructors stop trying to improve their management of the child's troubling behaviors. To be forgiven does not imply that one is free to commit the same mistakes over and over again. Allowing oneself to be objective about one's performance as a caregiver means letting go of feelings of self-deprecation, shame, embarrassment, resentment, and rage and replacing them with a determination to do better the next time around. Humanity faces an uphill battle when it comes to forgiving one another. This is the most difficult guideline for parents and caregivers to follow, but it is the most important when it comes to effectively and peacefully managing children with ADHD.

Chapter 6
Educational Approaches
for Boys

In a classroom, there are several distractions for students of all ages. It is difficult for students to focus on their work when they are distracted by other students, the corridor, or even the outside world. In addition, it is difficult for any student, let alone a youngster with ADHD, to sit still, keep quiet, and focus on one task at a time. The diagnosis of an ADHD child can be a major challenge for many parents. Even though no parent wants to see their child suffer, it is essential that parents come to terms with the truth. Accepting that your child has ADHD is the first step in providing the support he needs to be successful in school and in life. According to cultural assumptions, children with ADHD are just lazy and unintelligent, rather than being diagnosed with a serious mental illness. In the end, this is exactly what the youngsters will believe if their difficulties are ignored.

Here are several effective ways to assist your boy with **ADHD** to learn:

Seat your child in an area that is free of potential distractions.

Provide a place for your youngster to do his homework away from distractions like the television or siblings. Pets should be kept with other family members and in a separate room if you have one. This will allow them to concentrate without being distracted by loud or attention-grabbing stimuli.

To aid your boy's learning, strike a healthy balance between energetic and passive activities.

This could include sitting down and doing math homework. After completing this task, have your child do something that demands they move around, such as creating a collage, a poster, or conducting a science experiment. After a long period of sitting and concentrating, it is beneficial for a youngster to complete a chore that allows them to expend some energy. Although it may take your child a few minutes away from their work, this will help them regain their focus when they return to the activity at hand.

Allow frequent breaks for your child. Don't have your child do one project after another in a short period of time. Trying to finish your child's job without a break can cause your youngster to lash out, lose focus, or refuse to do it at all. To avoid this, give your youngster regular pauses. Allow your youngster 10 minutes of free play after each activity is completed (granting the opportunity to release more energy). You should avoid letting your child watch television for several reasons, including the fact that a TV show typically lasts at least 30 minutes, and it is very likely that a child will want to watch another episode or two and lose the desire and ability to return to his work area to finish the remaining work. Also, make sure your youngster takes regular breaks to drink water, use the restroom, or eat a snack (depending on the family schedule).

Another way to help a youngster with ADHD learn is to break down a large task into smaller ones.

Everybody has moments when a large task seems insurmountable and depressingly tough to complete. When it comes to making things smaller, parents have a crucial role to play. When a project lasts a week, have your youngster break it down into smaller and more manageable goals for each day. These goals should be clear, simple, and prominently displayed for your child's benefit. You may boost your child's self-esteem and help them achieve their goals by allowing them to cross off a goal when it is completed. In addition to large-scale initiatives, this can be used for daily tasks as well. As a parent, it's important to set a particular goal for your child so that he can concentrate on it. Once the prior one has been fulfilled, create a new objective for your youngster to work toward completing. Breaking an assignment into smaller parts allows your youngster to focus on each individual task rather than cramming everything into one big project.

Keep a stress ball or little bean bag in your child's hands at all times.

Hyperactivity can be alleviated with the use of this approach. Your child will be able to let off some steam if he has something to hold in his hands. You can help your youngster relax by giving them a stress ball to squeeze.

Assist your child in completing the task.

Don't bring up the fact that the child isn't focused. Direct inquiries like, "Can you show me how you would solve the next problem?" would help your child focus. How would you go about solving this problem? "I'd like to know how you accomplished it." Keeping your child involved in the activity will help to keep them engaged and on task for the duration of the lesson. Parent-child bonding is enhanced as a result of this activity. In addition to helping your child concentrate, you'll gain valuable insight into their cognitive process and how well they're doing academically. When it comes to helping your child with ADHD learn, redirection is a lifesaver. Do not assist your child with homework if you are easily frustrated and end up fighting with him.

Your child with ADHD will benefit from your example.

The best way to help your child with ADHD learn is to act out how you expect him to behave. If you want your youngster to begin working at the table, sit down first and get comfortable in your own chair. " Doing so will increase the chances of a future imitator of your actions. If you need to look something up while working with your child, do so and make sure your child is watching. Children will imitate their parents' behavior if they see you doing something that benefits them. You can make it easier for yourself to complete a word problem by breaking it down into manageable chunks while you work on it. Your child will be more likely to copy you if you are consistent in the actions you model for him.

To help your child learn, you might utilize positive reinforcement as another tool.

Praise your youngster when he exhibits behavior that is conducive to learning. To please their parents as well as themselves, children often engage in pleasurable actions that they find pleasurable and will repeat over and over again. When you notice your youngster working quietly or concentrating, compliment him. You can say something like, "I appreciate how quiet you are working," or "I think it's amazing that you took the time to display all your efforts on that division problem," etc. Specifying your positive comments encourages the same kind of conduct to be replicated in the future by letting children know exactly what they're being applauded for. Helping a child with ADHD isn't always going to be simple, but it's worth it. It is possible for children with ADHD to achieve academic and personal success if they are provided with the proper support and guidance. Take the time to find out what works best for your child's education. You'll find the most effective tactics if you pay attention to your child's unique learning style and requirements. Every child is unique, and what works for one may not work for the next. Always be patient, caring, and sensitive in order to help your child with ADHD learn.

Chapter 7
12 Effective Discipline Techniques

ADHD is a neurodevelopmental disease in children characterized by impulsive, hyperactive behavior and a short attention span. ADHD may be the cause of impulsive and hyperactive behavior in youngsters that goes on for a long period of time. Many parents of children with ADHD are baffled by how to deal with their child's ADHD-related behavior. A child's everyday activities and quality of life might be negatively impacted by ADHD. In addition, the child's behavior may also be distressing to those in its social context. As a result of this, it is of the utmost importance to create an efficient means of disciplining them. To help you better understand how to discipline and manage a child with ADHD, here is some practical advice and tactics.

Disciplining an ADHD child: A few practical pointers

In order to discipline an ADHD child, you don't have to modify your parenting methods completely. Instead, you'll need to put in the time and effort.

1. The keys to success are patience and perseverance. Children with ADHD are generally impulsive and have a hard time controlling their feelings. It's difficult for them to stick to a schedule. These individuals could have a more difficult time following instructions because of their difficulties with cognition, emotion, and conduct. Keep trying these things until you find something that works.

   - It is a worthwhile investment of your time to teach your child how to organize, and prioritize work.

   - Help your child stay organized by providing them with daily planners, checklists, and alarms.

   - After using an item, put it back in its proper place by instructing your youngster to do the same.

   - Assign your boy to minor activities related to organizing, prioritizing, and structuring so that he gains hands-on experience. This could include tasks such as setting the dinner table or arranging your living area according to a set of guidelines. Make sure you wait for the child to complete one activity before moving on to the next.

2. Listen and pay attention. Attention-seeking behavior in children with ADHD can wear you out. But it's the youngsters who are more likely to

become overwhelmed by the many events taking place around them. Keeping track of and exerting control over their immediate environment may prove to be a difficult task for them. Be patient and give them a chance to be alone with you. With this information, you will be more prepared.

- Ensure that they know that you have their back by instilling confidence in them.
- Draw attention to the areas in which the youngster needs to improve.
- Recognize how you and your child's parents can work together to improve their conduct.

Make sure your youngster understands that changing his behavior takes time and cannot be rushed. Also, refrain from interjecting when your child is speaking. When they ask you a question, pay attention and give a suitable answer.

3. Establish a schedule and make sure your youngster follows it. Setting rules and expectations that are understandable, reasonable, and doable for the youngster is the key here. As an example, you can create a set of house rules, such as no smoking in the house.

- Physical activity should be done for at least 30 minutes every day.

- Wake up early and go to sleep early in the day.
- Clean the room immediately after waking up

To help your child keep to a schedule, you need to remind them, praise them, and encourage them. Make certain that the rules of the house are consistently enforced and that the youngster adheres according to the schedule.

4. Minimize distractions. During mealtimes, schoolwork time, or during a conversation with you, switch off the television and music. Overstimulation can be avoided by doing this. You can also avoid busy places like malls if you have a young child with you. Make sure the television and video games in your child's room are disconnected.

5. Ensure effective communication. This is critical as children with ADHD frequently have difficulty following directions due to symptoms such as hyperactivity, inattention, or a combination of the two. For essential conversations with your child, find a quiet place where they won't be distracted. As soon as they've done that, ask them to sit calmly and look at you. Explain the situation to the youngster when they are sitting calmly. To ensure that your youngster is paying attention, have him repeat the directions to you. You can also split down your daily

duties and chores into manageable chunks for your children to follow. Provide a written checklist, for example, if you wish to ask your youngster to clear the table after dinner.

- Disinfect all of your used utensils in the dishwasher.
- Clean up after yourself by tossing dirty napkins in the hamper.
- Use a dish towel to wipe down the table.

Physical contact, such as a gentle pat on the shoulder or a pat on the hand, can be used to keep your child's attention and ensure that he understands what you've just explained to him.

6. The children should be praised for their hard work. Your child should be praised when they follow your instructions, such as when they sit still and study, play quietly with their siblings or friends, or show good behavior with their friends. For example, you could remark, "I'm really proud of you," or "You're such a good kid."

Make them feel valued and acknowledged by showering them with hugs, kisses, and tiny prizes in addition to the lovely words. As a final note, let your children know as soon as you notice good or bad behavior so that they can decide whether or not their activities are appropriate.

7. Positive behavior should be rewarded. Rewarding a child for good behavior is, according to experts, an effective way to keep them on track. Give them something they can hold onto, like a sheet of smiley face stickers, for when they do something good. There is a token economy system that you can follow as well.

- A privilege or reward is given to the child if they demonstrate good conduct, such as doing their homework on time or putting their books and toys in the appropriate location.
- The child's prizes or privileges are taken away if he displays unfavorable behavior. You may, for example, cut down on your TV usage by 20 minutes each night.

8. Use the "time-out" technique. Distracting the child for a period of time in order to teach desired conduct is the goal of this method of child discipline. For example, if a child is being disrespectful by throwing things at their siblings or otherwise disrupting the class, have them seated in a different part of the room. For a set amount of time, ignore their cries, whines, or tantrums. You might also find a quiet spot to unwind. It will give you and the child time to think and wonder. Put in the time-out rule only after you've gone over with

the kid what it means and what kinds of bad behavior deserve it.

9. Refrain from using punishment as a tool for behavior modification. Your efforts may be jeopardized if you yell, scream, or spank at your youngster. Do not lose your cool, and keep in mind that youngsters with ADHD are not intentionally misbehaving. Their incapacity to control themselves is what drives people to act in particular ways. With patience, dedication, and the correct direction, you can learn to handle the child's irregular behavior.

    Note: It is also not uncommon for youngsters with ADHD to also have signs of oppositional defiant disorder (ODD). ODD is characterized by a kid's deliberate defiance of authority figures, such as parents and teachers, who attempt to discipline the child in an effort to control the kid. According to experts, punishing such children can increase their negativity and pessimism.

10. Educate your students on the natural consequences of their actions. Do not continually remind your youngster to exercise caution or to consider the consequences of their actions before acting. Instead, give them the freedom to do as they choose and let them deal with the fallout. For example, if your child does poorly on a school test, you can request that they study for additional hours each

day. Remind them that their lack of concentration in class has a logical and unavoidable consequence: they will have to spend more time studying.

11. Let them take charge. Engage your child in the process of establishing acceptable behaviors and rewards. This aids a child in remembering what is required of them. You and your child can, for example, decide to refrain from using social media while studying. However, they can do so when they take a break from their studies. Children are more likely to follow regulations that have been agreed upon by both parents.

12. Work with teachers and school administrators. Keeping tabs on a child's conduct and communicating the areas in which they need to improve is an essential first step. Teacher support for the child's academics, such as allowing them to finish a task at their own pace, will also be made easier by this information.

As your child matures and adapts to your established rules, expectations, and routines, they become more self-directed. When your child is able to function on his own, you can progressively reduce the amount of support you provide. The development of a child's self-confidence and self-esteem depends on a sense of autonomy and responsibility.

Chapter 8
Students' Guide to Studying & Doing Homework

Study and Homework Help for Students with ADHD

Boys with ADHD face unique challenges when it comes to developing effective study habits. As parents, what can we do?

1. Be an Advocate

Be a strong voice for your child's interests. Meet with your child's teachers to go over any issues with homework. The teachers of your child may not be able to meet with you at all times. If this is the case, you can either email them or give them a call. Teachers have the discretion to reduce the amount of homework given to their kids if they see it as necessary. Your child may just have to complete problems 1 to 15 of the usual math assignment. Teachers can put this up in advance. Your child may also be granted additional time to finish assignments.

2. Provide tools and support.

Provide help and resources for others' use. Help your child choose a notebook in which to record their homework assignments by going shopping with them. See if the teachers will aid with verbal reminders to the whole class, "Your homework tonight is..." A few minutes each will be given. Now is the time to begin drafting your homework. " Aside from verbal directions, find out if teachers will start writing tasks on the board. This strategy can benefit not only your child but the entire class as a whole. Teachers can keep an eye on your child to make sure he is paying attention and writing down the homework in the correct manner. Otherwise, a gentle tap on the desk or a handshake may be all that's needed to bring them back on track without drawing undue attention to themselves. Teachers can even verify the accuracy of the homework notebook at the conclusion of the class. Consider getting a copy of the week's assignments so that you have them at home as a backup plan if necessary.

3. At Home, Keep the Second Set of Books.

See if you can get an extra set of schoolbooks to use at home throughout the school year by contacting the principal. Even bringing home the essential textbooks at the end of the school day may be a challenge for children with ADHD. When things go a little out of whack at home, having a backup set can be a godsend.

4. Organize the Backpack

Organize your child's backpack with their assistance. Instead of a half-eaten, rotting apple from a school snack two weeks ago, he will have a fresh one waiting for him. This will allow your child to organize their supplies and not be distracted by other objects in the bag. For a child with ADHD, your extra help and direction are essential, even if these chores appear simple at first.

5. Color Coding

The use of color labeling is crucial. The notebook you purchase for your boy's school assignments is a great opportunity to stock up on a variety of fun and brightly colored supplies. Each hue should be matched to a specific subject. Consider purchasing a dedicated homework binder. Your boy will be able to keep track of all his assignments in one convenient location rather than scrambling around in a jumble of papers in his backpack.

6. Scheme Homework Time

At the end of the day, it's a good idea to help your child with homework right away. After refueling with a snack and a drink, it's time for homework. Kids that need a little exercise and outside play can benefit from it. Just before homework time, give your boy a chance to let off some steam and go back to work. Rather than your child's bedroom, designate a space for homework that is away from the main living areas of your home. There may be too many distractions in that location. You may feel more alone in your bedroom.

In order to help your child, you should always be accessible to answer questions and offer suggestions. Some youngsters thrive in a calm environment. A little music or background noise may help some kids concentrate better. Periodic, brief breaks are helpful for some students. You and your child can figure out together what kind of atmosphere is most conducive to their learning and development. Assist your child in developing a routine that is predictable and devoid of anxiety. After your boy has finished his homework, double-check it. Once the task is finished, assist your kid in zipping up their homework folder and returning all necessary supplies to their book bag.

7. Medication

If a child is taking medication, it's possible that the medication's effects will wear off by the time homework time rolls around in the late afternoon. Ask your child's doctor whether it is possible to arrange for one of the medications to be taken later in the day to aid with homework time. Your child's sleep may be disrupted if he takes medicine late at night.

8. Praise

Try to keep a positive attitude when doing schoolwork. Give your child a pat on the back for their good effort during this time. Congratulate them on their efforts in front of the rest of the family. It's so easy to dwell on the negative at times. Remember to praise your child for his accomplishments. If everything goes according to plan, reward your boy at the end of the week by taking him out for some quality time.

9. Set Up A Homework-Only Room

A child with ADHD is easily distracted by their environment. Place your child in a quiet, distraction-free environment where he can concentrate. Use this as a peaceful study area where your youngster can clear his head and focus away from noise and movement.

10. Create a Consistent Schedule

It is critical for children with ADHD to adhere to a regular schedule. A good place to start for your child is with their schoolwork. Allow your child to work at a designated time each day.

11. Studying in Spurts

Breaks are essential for those with ADHD who have trouble concentrating. In order to get the most out of your boy's time studying, it is best to break it up into short periods of time. Make sure your child takes regular breaks from schoolwork to eat something or go for a stroll, and allow their minds to recharge. This will allow your youngster to burn off surplus energy and increase concentration when he returns.

12. Getting the Teacher Involved

It's difficult to keep up with what your child is doing in school. Make sure you're informed by talking to your child's teacher. Ask the teacher whether you can receive periodic reports and updates on your child's homework from them. It's best if you can set up a meeting with them every few weeks to check in on their development. If you and your child's teacher are aware of what is happening in the classroom, you may make adjustments to ensure that your child is learning effectively.

13. Get Organized

Get school supplies organized and set up schedules and checklists for completing homework and other tasks. Your child's school bag should be prepared the night before, and all homework should be completed. Colored folders, special pencils, stickers, and custom labels may make organizing fun for your child.

14. Show Support

You can help your child succeed by encouraging him to always do his best. When your youngster asks for aid, it's fine to lend a helping hand. In order to help your child, stay motivated, teach him to see obstacles as opportunities for growth. Show that you are constantly there to help him succeed.

15. Acknowledge Your Child's Learning Processes

It's critical to understand your child's preferred method of learning, be it aural, kinesthetic, or visual. Visuals, music, exercising, or talking out loud can all be used to help students adjust their study habits to their preferred method of learning. Each child learns in a unique way. Studying in a style that works best for the student might aid in retention and comprehension.

16. When It's Time to Stop

Children with ADHD are prone to becoming annoyed and overwhelmed. As long as your child is able to encourage them to keep going as long as they can. Stop for the night if he has reached their limit. Send a note to the teacher if the following day's homework isn't finished.

17. Provide compliments and appreciation.

Congratulations on a job well done! Tell your child how proud you are. You may also plan a special outing, such as a trip to the park or a modest treat. The next day, set a new goal for your child, even if he didn't finish the one they started.

18. Move Around

Students with ADHD may find it difficult to sit still for long periods of time. Allowing your child to get up and move around can aid in concentration. Counting steps while practicing math problems like addition and subtraction can be a fun way to help your child learn. Having something with which to occupy his hands while working can also be beneficial. Taking a stress ball with you wherever you go is a terrific idea for your child.

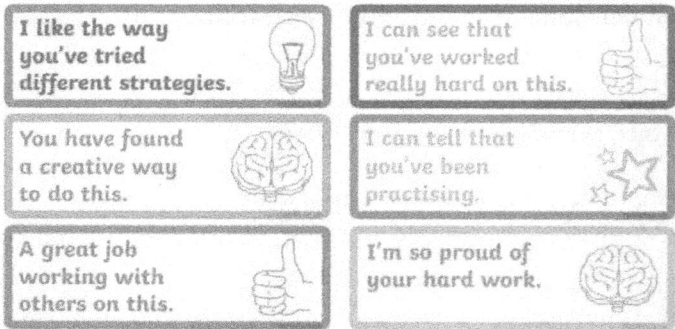

I like the way you've tried different strategies.	I can see that you've worked really hard on this.
You have found a creative way to do this.	I can tell that you've been practising.
A great job working with others on this.	I'm so proud of your hard work.

Photo Credit: www.piggyride.com

19. Give Verbal Feedback and Rewards

When your child completes their schoolwork on time, give them a pat on the back. It takes a long time and a lot of pampering, feedback, and encouragement to help an ADHD youngster focus. Tell them things like, "I'm proud of you," "You're intelligent," "You're doing a fantastic job," and other positive statements. Words have power and meaning. Kids will feel better about themselves if you give them positive comments. Motivating children with ADHD and making them feel important is an excellent way to do this. Consider complimenting their efforts rather than condemning them. If they think you don't appreciate what they've done, they may get aggressive. Regular prizes like an extra hour of gaming time, their favorite ice cream, an extra hour of playing, etc., should also be offered. Also, it will inspire students to finish their schoolwork.

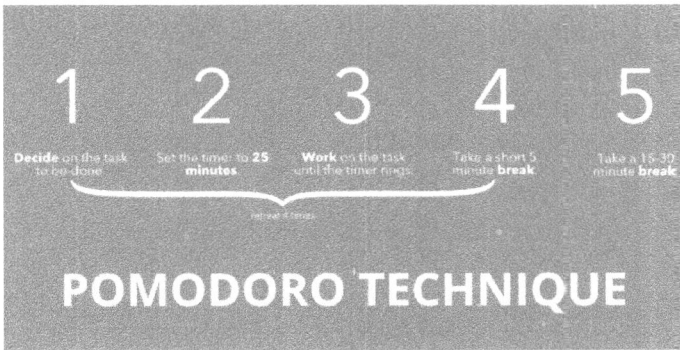

Photo Credit: www.piggyride.com

20. Present the POMODORO study Method.

Because they can't concentrate for more than 30 minutes at a time, helping an ADHD child with homework is no easy task. Children can benefit greatly from the POMODORO study method. With this method, kids can take regular rests while also being able to concentrate better.

What exactly is the Pomodoro method?

1. Choose an upcoming homework assignment.
2. Set a timer for twenty-five minutes.
3. Work until the timer goes off.
4. Take a 5-minute break!
5. Repeat this procedure thrice.
6. After completing four cycles, take a 15- to 30-minute break.

Chapter 9
Diet for Your ADHD Boy

The Importance of a Kid's ADHD Diet

Just like kids without ADHD, children with ADHD must reach the same milestones as their peers: learning, growing, and experiencing the world around them. However, children with ADHD may also face the following difficulties: Anorexia, obsessive-compulsive disorder (OCD), and other eating disorders. It's no surprise that effective therapy for ADHD necessitates proper nutrition. An ADHD diet paired with medicine can help youngsters improve their ability to study, pay attention, and decrease any impulsive tendencies or hyperactivity. In addition, a healthy diet aids your child's physical and mental well-being.

ADHD and children's nutrition are intertwined.

Children with ADHD benefit from a well-balanced diet rich in whole foods and nutrients. Reduce the amount of sugar, artificial colors, and other ingredients that you use. Despite this, children with ADHD are plagued by fussy eating, impulsive eating, and recurrent dietary behaviors. Even when a child with ADHD isn't hungry, he should be fed on a regular schedule to ensure that the child receives appropriate nutrients throughout the day. Having regular meals and snacks can improve a child's attention span, conduct, hunger, and growth. Finally, a diet for ADHD patients emphasizes interactions at the table that are upbeat and supportive.

In this case study, we'll look at a young boy with ADHD.

Peter (real name altered) suffered from ADHD. He was quite underweight, ate terribly, and was a finicky eater to boot. His diet consisted primarily of white dishes, and he rarely ate any fruits or vegetables. He was content with anything crunchy, cheesy, salty, or sweet. A daily dose of medicine, which reduced Peter's desire for food, began after he was diagnosed. Most of his meals occurred at the end of the day on several occasions. Those were the days when his drugs began to wear off and he was hungry. Helping Peter's mother in the following areas was requested:

- Persuade him to eat more vegetables.
- Encourage him to try different foods
- Assist him in gaining weight and addressing his thinness

She wanted (and needed) to help Peter move to a diet that was more conducive to his ADHD symptoms. In order for Peter to get the nutrition he required, he had to change his diet. He wasn't eating enough, and his eating habits were all over the place. As a result, his development, demeanor, and ability to concentrate in class were all suffering, making it difficult for him to study.

ADHD and nutrients

The formative years of a person's life lay a solid basis for their health as an adult. A growing body of evidence suggests that improving a child's diet helps alleviate the symptoms of ADHD. For example, nutrients are necessary for the brain to function properly. A well-balanced diet provides the brain with all the nutrients it needs to perform at its best, from complex carbohydrates to heart-healthy fats. Children with ADHD who eat a healthy, well-balanced diet may be better able to concentrate, behave, and get along with others. In addition, a healthy diet can aid your child's development and may help prevent chronic problems in the future. Sadly, research has shown that some children with ADHD do not get enough of certain nutrients in their diets, and this can have an impact on their ability to concentrate, conduct appropriately, and develop normally.

ADHD, medication, and appetite

It's not always easy to eat healthily. When a child has ADHD, there are several challenges to eating healthily. For example, several ADHD drugs might reduce your child's appetite, resulting in less food being consumed.

It's possible that your child will lose their appetite completely while taking these medications. When he is no longer taking medication, he may eat a lot. Some drugs have been found to be the cause of stomach pain or nausea, which can be so distressing for children that they refuse to eat.

Sensory issues, ADHD, and picky eaters

Picky eating is another hindrance to a healthy diet. Picky eating might be the result of an innate aversion to certain tastes, textures, or appearances, or it can develop as a result of inefficient strategies and feeding errors. Your child's picky eating habits could be preventing him from receiving the proper nutrition. Of course, the roadblocks don't end there. Feeding your child may be a genuine hardship and a significant stressor for families when they pile up on top of each other.

ADHD Nutrition for Children

Personally, I've seen the positive impact that a healthy food system and feeding methods can have on children with ADHD. They have a more positive outlook on life and perform better as a result. As we understand more about the dietary requirements of children with ADHD, we are better able to identify the nutrients and foods that can be beneficial to these children. Included in an ADHD diet are various nutrients you'll want to keep an eye on, along with an optimum caloric intake and frequent food options. Ensuring that your child receives enough to eat and improving his appetite can both be made easier with this kind of attention. Your child can consume foods that are good for ADHD, but your child can also eat foods that are bad for ADHD.

ADHD Diets: Is There a Standardized One?

Even while eating isn't thought to be a cause of ADHD, many health experts believe that nutrition can help manage the disorder. Individual studies have examined the effects of certain diets on brain function and attentiveness. Changing your child's diet to better control their ADHD can be done in a variety of ways.

High Nutrition

Increasing your child's intake of nutrients such as iron, magnesium, and vitamin D will help ensure that they get all the vitamins and minerals they require, as low mineral levels have been linked to ADHD symptoms in children. Regardless of whether your child has ADHD or not, ensuring that he consumes adequate amounts of foods that contain these nutrients is a good idea in general.

Elimination

Elimination diets are frequently used to determine if a person is sensitive to certain foods. It entails temporarily avoiding the majority of common foods before gradually reintroducing them one at a time. When you reintroduce a food after a period of abstinence, the hope is that you'll be able to identify the culprit. If you suspect that specific foods are contributing to your child's ADHD symptoms, this is an option worth exploring. Research suggests that it may be extremely effective.

Supplementation

It's not always easy to get kids to eat healthy foods like fruits and vegetables. Because of this, some parents prefer to supplement their children's diets with vitamins and minerals to ensure that they are getting all the nutrients they need. A medical expert should be consulted before giving your child vitamins. A nutritionist that specializes in ADHD diets can be a good choice because she or he has likely done much research on the subject.

How Effective is an ADHD-Focused Diet?

It is possible that an ADHD diet can benefit children with ADHD. An ADHD diet can help regulate ADHD in children, even if you don't go through the hassle of a full exclusion diet, by boosting your child's vitamin and mineral intake, or simply providing your child with high-quality, nutritional food.

If you have a child who suffers from ADHD, the following dietary groups are recommended. Of course, you must also take care to feed your child foods that are compatible with their allergies and sensitivities.

Protein

ADHD symptoms can be reduced by feeding children an ADHD-specific protein, such as whey protein. Whey protein comes from cows and may be polluted with herbicides or pesticides. Pasture-raised, grass-fed, organic products are the best option. Alternatively, you can substitute plant-based protein for animal protein. Protein is the most recommended macronutrient for children with ADHD. Our bodies can produce the neurotransmitters necessary for concentration, focus, and relaxation when we eat protein-rich foods.

Protein-Rich Foods

- Eggs
- Meats like poultry and lean beef fish
- Nuts
- Beans

Complex Carbohydrates

Serotonin is released in the brain when complex carbohydrates are consumed in their natural form. The neurotransmitter serotonin is involved in mood regulation. Serotonin is released by all carbohydrates, but complex carbohydrates have more fiber since they are left in their natural form. Our bodies produce serotonin at a slower rate when we eat more fiber. This will help you avoid experiencing sudden highs and lows in your mood.

Complex Carbohydrate Foods

- Whole grains (e.g., brown rice and quinoa)
- Root vegetables (e.g., sweet potatoes and beets)

Omega-3 Fatty Acids

Children with ADHD have low levels of essential fatty acids (PUFAs). The term "essential" refers to nutrients that your child's body cannot produce on its own. To meet your child's needs for these fatty acids, they must be obtained outside the body. In addition to fish and some nut and vegetable oils, polyunsaturated fatty acids (PUFAs) are also found in animal fats, such as olive, canola, and safflower oils. PUFAs aid in the circulation of blood to the brain. Eicosatetraenoic acid (EPA), a type of fatty acid known to enhance cerebral blood flow, has been shown to be safe and effective. A number of studies have indicated that EPA can lessen the signs and symptoms of ADHD, including hyperactivity and impulsivity. You don't have to worry about your child's health if he eats a diet rich in plant fats and seafood. Docosahexaenoic acid (DHA) is an essential fatty acid for nerve cell activity. Supplementing with a combination of EPA and DHA may help children with ADHD operate better overall. The following sources of Omega-3 Fatty Acids are best obtained:

- Flaxseed and chia seeds
- Soybeans and tofu
- Cod liver oil.
- Coldwater fish (i.e., salmon, mackerel, tuna, and sardines)
- Walnuts
- Plant-based foods (e.g., flax seeds, walnuts, chia seeds, and soybeans)

What Foods Should Your Child Stay Away From?

When it comes to treating and preventing ADHD in children, the above-mentioned foods have been proven to be beneficial, but the foods listed below have the opposite impact.

Carbohydrates that are refined and simple

Carbohydrates that have been refined lose some of their nutrients, making them less nutritious than unprocessed versions. Children with ADHD find sugar the most problematic, and those who limit their intake show fewer signs of ADHD. Our bodies manufacture serotonin when we eat refined carbs like white flour, but the lack of fiber prevents that release from being slow and constant. Instead, they cause a rapid rise and fall in blood sugar levels. A wide variety of commercial snack items, from chips to crackers to fruit snacks, are made with refined carbohydrates. More processed foods are linked to an increased risk of ADHD in the general population.

Caffeine

For parents of children with ADHD, it may be tempting to allow their children to consume caffeine-containing beverages like coffee, tea, and many sodas and energy drinks. Avoid doing this. To make matters worse, caffeine has been shown to have severe negative effects on children's ADHD drugs. It can also cause jitteriness and anxiety, which are undesirable side effects.

Food Additives

An increase in ADHD symptoms in youngsters has been linked to food dyes in a number of studies. The behavior and neurology of youngsters might be adversely affected by both red and yellow. It has not been established that food additives cause ADHD, but some research has shown that food additives negatively impact child behavior, including that of children with ADHD. It's best to stay away from processed foods and opt for healthy foods with fewer ingredients. This involves selecting items that list the majority of (if not all) of their ingredients as food. Food additives are the chemical-sounding terms at the end of nutrition labels that are difficult to describe but can be found in processed foods. Sodium benzoate and red color #40 are two examples.

The most important nutrients for treating ADHD

The following are some of the most important nutrients for treating ADHD:

Fiber and ADHD

A lack of fiber in a child's diet is a common symptom of ADHD. To a large extent, this is due to a lack of fruits and vegetables in a person's diet. Fruits and vegetables, nuts, seeds, and whole grains like brown rice or whole grain pasta are excellent sources of fiber for children's diets. If your child has a problem with constipation, you'll want to make sure they're receiving enough fiber and water in their diets.

Magnesium

This vital trace mineral plays a key role in the body's enzymatic processes, where it is involved in more than 300 reactions. Magnesium is essential to a wide range of metabolic functions. Among these are the metabolism and formation of bone tissue, the activity of nerves; the release of neurotransmitters; the operation of the immune system; and the control of the hypothalamic-pituitary-adrenal axis. There has been a correlation between low magnesium levels in children with ADHD and autism. Children with ADHD may be particularly sensitive if they have a deficiency in magnesium. In young people, magnesium deficiency can cause irritability, anxiety, and agitation. Anxiety and irritation are reduced by magnesium's soothing impact. Magnesium-rich Foods:

- Spinach
- Squash & pumpkin seeds
- Brown rice
- Avocados
- Bananas
- Low-fat dairy
- Fish
- Beans and lentils
- Dried fruits such as apricots, dates, figs, prunes, and raisins.

Iron and ADHD

Poor cognitive development is linked to a lack of iron in the diet, especially in the first few years of life. The brain may not develop to its full intellectual potential if it suffers from an iron deficit throughout its formative years. Additional long-term effects of iron deficiency include weakened immunity, exhaustion, and difficulty learning in later life. Symptoms of iron deficiency can appear in children with ADHD. Symptoms of an iron deficiency include insomnia and restless leg syndrome. Symptoms can occur even when iron levels are at or near the lower end of the normal range in children. Children with ADHD, particularly those who are finicky eaters, are a cause for concern. They may not be eating enough iron-rich foods like beef, poultry, beans, and dark leafy greens. An iron deficit that has been documented should be treated with supplements under the supervision of your healthcare physician. A healthcare expert can help you determine the proper dosage of iron because too much iron can be dangerous. Children with ADHD who are not iron deficient may not benefit from iron supplements.

Foods Rich in Iron:

- Red meat, pork, and poultry
- Chickpeas
- Spinach
- Raisins and apricots
- Seafood
- Beans and lentils
- Peas

Zinc and ADHD

Zinc, like iron, has a role in the formation of the brain, the transmission of nerve signals, and other functions of the brain. Zinc deficiency has been linked to inattention in children with ADHD (but not impulsivity or hyperactivity). Zinc deficiency has been linked to poor growth and an inability to eat. If your kid has zinc deficiency, you should get it taken care of by giving him a supplement. Consuming foods high in zinc, such as beans, meat, fortified cereals, and milk, is critical for maximizing zinc absorption.

Folate and ADHD

In spite of the fact that a great number of grain products have folate added to them, Western diets as a whole, and certain people in particular, do not consume enough folate. Foods high in folate have been recommended for children with ADHD as part of a healthy diet.

Avoid Eating These Foods

ADHD-related behaviors have been linked to certain diets. <u>Fast food, processed meats, potato chips, and other snack foods are all included in this category.</u> These are the kinds of foods that, in moderation, can be included in your child's diet. You can gradually cut down the amount of fast food and other processed items in your child's diet. Food additives, such as MSG, nitrates, nitrites, and artificial sugar, can also cause reactions or sensitivities in children with ADHD. According to research, about 8% of children with ADHD may be allergic to artificial food colorings. It's possible that the figure is higher than previously thought.

What about sugar and ADHD?

Some parents feel that children with ADHD are more prone to hyperactivity because they consume a lot of sugar. A high-sugar diet is bad for everyone, but it's especially bad for kids. Childhood obesity, tooth decay, and type-2 diabetes have been linked to a child's high sugar intake. Therefore, limiting your child's sugar consumption is a good idea, even if it does not directly affect their behavior.

How to Feed an ADHD Child

Structure, boundaries, and guided choices are all important when it comes to feeding children with ADHD. A child's behavior, focus, and ability to study all suffer when he goes without food for long periods of time.

Do you have an underweight ADHD child?

Experts recommend more frequent meals and snacks during the day. Even if your child will only eat one piece of cheese or cracker for breakfast and one piece of fruit for lunch, their behavior, attentiveness, and overall energy and optimism will all benefit from regular small feedings.

Positive Atmosphere at Mealtime

It can be a challenge to feed an ADHD child. In the course of daily life, you may face behavioral, eating, and other issues. Don't put too much pressure on yourself when it comes to eating and feeding.

Foods That Can Help Treat or Prevent ADHD

A specific cuisine does not cure or alleviate ADHD symptoms, but different diets have been linked to the condition. A Mediterranean diet rich in whole grains, legumes, fruits, vegetables, and seafood appears to have the opposite effect of a Western diet high in fat and refined sugar. When it comes to their children's nutrition, parents should focus on providing a balanced diet. Foods from several food groups and the following nutrients should be included in an ADHD diet that is well-balanced.

Complex carbohydrates

Whole grains and cereals are other good sources of complex carbohydrates.

Lean protein

An essential component of the human body's machinery, proteins play an important role in everything from cell regeneration to enzyme manufacturing. Increase your child's protein intake by including beans, lentils, tofu, and low-fat dairy products, as well as egg whites, poultry, and fish. The protein needs of children between the ages of four and 14 range from 19 to 46 grams per day.

Healthy fats

Fats should account for 25–35% of a child's total daily energy intake between the ages of four and 14 years old. Saturated fats should make up less than 10% of the total, while the rest should come from unsaturated fats. There are a number of reasons why fat is necessary for humans; one of them is that it aids in the absorption of fat-soluble vitamins A through K. As a result, children should be given the proper amounts of unsaturated fats like MUFA and PUFA. Include omega-3 fatty acids, which may aid in the relief of ADHD symptoms. Omega-3 fatty acids can be found in a variety of foods.

- Seeds, such as chia and flax seeds
- Nuts, such as walnuts
- Fatty fish (tuna and salmon)

What You Should Know Before Feeding an ADHD Diet to Your Child

Many parents find it difficult to organize and manage their child's food when caring for a child with ADHD. If you have a child with ADHD, you might find these helpful hints to help you plan their diet and promote healthy eating habits.

1. Follow a routine: Planning, organizing, and scheduling can be difficult for children with ADHD. Routines are a smart way to keep children on track. Serve meals at the same time every day if you want to see how that works for you. Children will look forward to eating if the foods are visually appealing and flavorful.

2. Never skip meals: It is essential that children get frequent, well-balanced meals. These meals should be prepared with your child in mind so that he understands the versatility and importance of each ingredient.

3. Ensure that your child is getting a well-rounded diet: Healthy foods from a variety of dietary groups make up a well-balanced meal. The macro-and micronutrients found in whole grain cereals, fruits, vegetables, nuts, and low-fat dairy products, for example, are essential for children's growth and development. Consider what your child eats and how you might make it healthy.

4. Beware of highly processed foods, which are often rich in fat and sugar content. Artificial colors and preservatives, for example, might affect your child's behavior if added to their diet. Encourage your child to consume more nutritious options. Provide

him with nutritious and substantial snacks. Provide your child with the following nutritious options:

- Fruits of the season include bananas, dragon fruits, plums, peaches, apples, papaya, and nectarines.
- Homemade smoothies and shakes, low-fat, sugar-free yogurt with fruit
- Crunchy chickpeas
- Dried fruits with no added sugar
- Air-popped, unsalted popcorn.
- Baked vegetables
- Nut and seed trail mix
- Fiber-rich cereals with dried fruits and nuts
- Whole-grain potato chips

Whatever nutritious snacks you decide to offer your child, be sure to give them a choice of two to three and allow them to make their own selections. Next, ensure that your child has ready access to their favorite meals so that they can eat them whenever they want.

5. The best thing you can do as a parent is to serve as an example for your child. So, model healthy eating habits for your child and encourage him to do the same. If you're eating at home or at a restaurant, opt for lean meat, fish, vegetables, and whole grain products. Eat as a family as often as you can to give

your children a taste of wholesome, home-cooked meals. This will also allow you to spend more time together as a family.

6. Your child should be taught to read food labels, as many store-bought products include unhealthy substances. In order to make well-informed decisions, it's critical to read food labels. When you go grocery shopping, take your boy along and show him how to read and interpret food labels. Trans fats, excessive sodium, and additives such as artificial colors and dyes should be avoided, as should refined carbohydrates, sugar, and other sugar substitutes. Take the advice of a nutritionist.

7. An ADHD-specific nutritionist (dietician) can help you design a diet plan for your child. Additional benefits include helping a child with ADHD discover, analyze, and correct their nutritional concerns. As an additional benefit, they can help you decide if you should supplement your child's diet with dietary or nutritional supplements.

Precautions

Allergens

Children with ADHD often have food sensitivities and intolerances, particularly to foods containing salicylates (such as tomatoes and grapes) and common allergens like peanuts, shellfish, wheat, milk, and soy. Some people find relief by avoiding the allergens they're sensitive to. This should only be done under the supervision of a pediatrician, as some children with ADHD are not allergic to or sensitive to particular foods.

Chapter 10
Strategies to Manage ADHD Behaviors (Part 1)

Dealing with an ADHD child can be difficult for parents. You want your child to reach his greatest potential, so you need to have the skills and strategies to keep things under control so he can live a normal life.

Strategy #1 Adjusting Your Residence's Environment For Your Child

What does it mean when you say you are going to alter your child's environment?

You may be able to modify your child's behavior by modifying his environment. This does not require a move, new furnishings, or the purchase of expensive play equipment. The behavioral environment includes the following:

- His location in the park, at home, or in a store
- Anything you don't want him to play with, including toys, books, and playground equipment
- By seeing the conduct of other children
- Sensations include sound and illumination

- Duration of the day
- Your requests and guidelines

These circumstances can have an impact on your child's conduct, and they can even occasionally provoke unwanted behavior. It is fairly common for your child to engage in the following behaviors:

Here are some suggestions for altering your child's physical surroundings to encourage the behavior you desire.

- He desires to have fun with the stuff in his surroundings.
- Determine more about his location
- Naptime causes him to feel sleepy.
- If there is a great deal of activity or noise, he may become overwhelmed.
- He is unwilling to part with his most valued possessions.
- If he cannot decipher your instructions, he will disregard them.

At home

- Dispose of fragile or precious items out of the way and out of the reach of children.
- A "quiet spot" should be designated for your child when they are feeling overwhelmed. For

instance, your child's favorite books and a certain cushion may suffice.

- When your child has to focus on an important task, such as getting ready for school in the morning, switch off electronic devices such as iPads and televisions.

Away from home

- If you have access to a secure outside location, such as a courtyard, playground, or backyard, take advantage of it. You will experience less anxiety, and those who observe your child's activities will have fewer complaints.

- Rotate seating configurations to ensure the comfort of all passengers, whether traveling by car, train, or bus. Place a parent in the middle of a table with two children as an example. It is also possible to allow one child to sit by the window for a period of time before switching.

- You and your child will appreciate the playground and coffee cart during a family outing.

- To alter the ambiance while driving, listen to music. If your child appears bored, play upbeat music, and if you want him to rest, play soothing music.

Toys and belongings

- With a child gate, the door to an older sibling's room can be secured. A younger sibling will not be able to interfere with the older child's playtime.
- Place your child's favorite toys in an accessible location. This will prevent him from climbing or entering hazardous circumstances while searching for his toys.
- Assist your child in determining which toys he does not like to share with other children and storing them.

Rearranging activities to better accommodate your child's timetable

You have the ability to affect your child's environment by shifting the order of occurrences. Consider the following:

- Start the evening with calm, peaceful activities such as reading or listening to relaxing music.
- After your child's nap, you should go grocery shopping with him.
- Rise early in the morning to reduce the stress associated with hurriedly getting to school on time.
- Start the timer sooner if you want to avoid a bath-time tantrum.

- It is advisable to take frequent breaks when driving for an extended period of time.

You may be able to affect your child's conduct by modifying the way his teacher asks him to do specific chores. When you tell your child to do something, you are providing them with instructions. For example, "please take and hold my hand when we cross the street." Children, on the other hand, may get angry or disobedient if given an excessive number of instructions. When you request something from your child, you are making a request. Please set the table for us. Your child can respond to a request with either "yes" or "no."

Strategy #2 Offering clear and concise instructions

Providing children with clear instructions and requests is vital for their cooperation. Instructions and requests should be interspersed in order to encourage children to collaborate. Providing excellent instructions and making an attempt to maintain your child's interest can assist in ensuring his attentiveness. Examples:

- Move in close to him.
- Lower yourself to your child's eye level.
- Refer to him by name.
- Use a deep and tranquil tone of voice.

- Request that your youngster repeats back to you what you just said.

Here are some other points:

- Use straightforward language
- Be positive
- Provide options while providing instructions. For instance, it is now dinner time. Choose between spinach and broccoli
- Prepare yourself to repeat yourself
- Apply the consequences

Teach your child the significance of paying close attention and following instructions. Tips:

- Continue to use the same familiar words.
- As soon as your child complies, provide him with positive reinforcement.
- Establish a regular program and adhere to it.
- You can encourage your child to participate in activities by making them entertaining or by including a game.

When your child may be uncooperative

Your child may need to be taught or demonstrate new abilities in order for him to cooperate. There may be a valid explanation for why your child is disobeying your requests. Consistency, firmness, and affection are essential while attempting to persuade a child to do what you desire.

Strategy #3 Reward and acknowledge positive conduct.

Your child's acts or behavior merit praise, such as "Good job, Paul," "Well done, John!" or "Wow, that's incredible." A child's self-esteem and confidence in their talents are bolstered by praise. Some children may require more assistance than others, particularly those with less self-confidence. As a parent, you can encourage your child to strive more in the future by complimenting their efforts. If children are praised for their hard work, they are more likely to view it as a positive trait.

The purpose of a reward is to commend your child for a job well done or excellent behavior. As an incentive for keeping his room clean, it could be a good idea to let your child choose what he will eat for supper. Initially, you can applaud each instance of the action or effort, but if it does not occur frequently enough, you may need to stop providing additional praise. It is prudent to avoid overusing rewards. If you often utilize them, it may be time to reevaluate your circumstances.

Consider nonverbal ways to express your approval of your child's conduct or efforts, such as a thumbs up, a smile, or a high five. Your child deserves a reward for good behavior: "Thank you for clearing the table—let's celebrate by going to the park!" Communicate to your children how proud you are of their achievements and how much they mean to you. Your child's self-esteem and pride will increase as a result. Your child might not believe you if you exaggerate your praise.

Strategy #4 Create daily routines.

Creating and adhering to routines is an efficient method for maintaining order in the home, as they specify who is responsible for each duty and when it must be accomplished. Establishing the practice of having your child independently peruse books prior to chanting or playing "I spy" or "alphabet hunt" is simple. Children are more likely to behave appropriately if they are well-rested, well-fed, and have ample opportunity to play.

A family schedule can help you manage your child's behavior and give them something to do while you complete household chores. Before and after school and work, these are the busiest times of the day for a family. For example, your child can comprehend, "We eat dinner early on Thursdays so that you will be on time for gymnastics class." Saying "We only watch a half-hour of television" to a toddler who does not know time can be perplexing.

Why is it so difficult to urge your child to adhere to a schedule? Some suggestions

- Make it easy for your child to adhere to the schedule independently. Install an alarm clock in your child's room so that they know when to wake up and get ready for school in the morning.
- A poster depicting your daily routine should be widely displayed in your home. Make it easy for your child to adhere to the schedule independently. Your child can gain valuable experience and contribute to the family by performing household responsibilities

Give your child a pat on the back when they complete a daily activity without your aid.

Strategy #5 The Coin Game

Many children who have ADHD struggle with impulse control, focus, processing speed, memory, and following directions. The good news is that you can help your child who has trouble focusing improve.

The Coin Game

Parents adore this game because it improves their children's memory, sequencing, and overall concentration. Because it is lively and fast-paced, it is a huge hit with children. You will need a small collection of coins, a cardboard sheet to cover them, and a stopwatch or timer app on your smartphone to begin. Take five coins from the stack, such as three pennies and two nickels, and arrange them in a logical manner. Now, instruct your child to carefully inspect the coins on the table.

Then, cover the coins with cardboard. Start the timer and see how long it takes them to construct the same pattern using coins from the pile. Remove the cardboard cover and set the timer to indicate when they will be finished. Record how long it took them to complete the task and whether or not it was completed the first time correctly. You should encourage your youngster to try again if the first attempt is unsuccessful. Include pennies, nickels, dimes, quarters, and half dollars to increase the complexity of the designs. Your child's attention span and ability to follow directions will improve as they play more, which is a tremendous benefit for both of you.

Strategy #6- Positive Visualization and Relaxation

The enhancement of existing abilities as well as the learning of new ones can be facilitated by including in one's daily routine such practices as meditation and relaxation, as well as positive visual imagery such as deep breathing. According to research, the brain of a child records fictional experiences in the same way as if they were true experiences, which results in an enhancement in the child's overall quality of life. Children who have ADHD may fool themselves into thinking that they are paying attention in class or coping with mocking, which may drive them to behave differently while at school. In other words, these children may confuse themselves into believing that they are paying attention. You and your child are able to put your creative energies to use by giving this a try.

Strategy #7 - High-Tech Aids for Your Child with ADHD

Graphical clock

If you have difficulty keeping track of the hours, one of them will be ideal: a watch representing the passage of time through a diminishing red disc.

Keyless lock

There are keyless door locks, such as those that utilize numerical codes or fingerprints. These gadgets may be made more secure while remaining simple to use because they can be easily updated with a new passcode or fingerprint.

Fail-safe alarm watch

To ensure that they wake up, many people with ADHD set their alarm clock on the opposite side of their bedroom from their bed.

Goof-proof garage door closer

If you forget to close the garage door, there is an app on SmartHome.com that can automatically close it for you.

Key finder

These are more than simply keys. The remote control for the television, eyeglasses and the phone handset are a few examples of items that can be located.

Intelligent watch

They can be beneficial for ADHD patients. Moreover, some gadgets include many alarms. By setting alarms every 15 to 30 minutes, you may hone your sense of timing.

Strategy #8 - The Fidgeter

What benefits do fidget spinners have for children?

Toys that revolve in a circle are both entertaining and prevalent. People display a series of behaviors known as fidgeting while doing everything from sitting and reading to addressing a massive crowd. It is a common method for releasing tension or energy. The manufacturers of fidget spinners assert that their products can be used to treat youngsters with ADHD. The toy's rhythmic motion may offer some relief to children with anxiety.

Fidget spinners may be useful!

One of the profs gave a personal insight.

One of my students is permitted to use a fidget spinner, which is acceptable to me. Due to his severe ADHD and behavioral problems, he is unable to attend classes in the main classroom. The fidget spinner enabled him to express some of his pent-up tensions without disturbing his classmates. I was astonished the first time he utilized it. He remained silent while he sat there. He was observant. He participated actively in the conversation. This fidget spinner was spinning the entire time continuously.

Remember, fidget spinners will not work miracles. The effectiveness of fidget spinners is inferior to that of sedatives and other treatments. This treatment is less disruptive than others, such as playing music, which can be distracting to others. Medication can also cause drowsiness, decreased judgment, and impaired reflex coordination, among other undesirable effects. Consider putting a fidget spinner to the test at school if your child's behavior changes at home appear to be beneficial. You can ensure your child receives the finest possible education with the assistance of the teacher. If you have concerns about whether a particular activity will be useful for your child, discuss your concerns with the teacher.

Strategy #9 - Listening to Directions

It may be frustrating to have a child that refuses to listen. Some parents respond by performing the task themselves, while others scold or nag their children until they comply. If your youngster does not follow your instructions the first time, you should reread them. These frequent errors can impair your child's listening skills:

A large number of orders

You likely give your child hundreds of instructions every day, from "Pick up your socks" to "Stop banging your fork on the table." Insisting that your youngster "color within the lines" and "pull up your socks" will irritate them. Your voice will fade into the background if you continue to offer advice and warnings on insignificant things. Avoid giving your youngster superfluous, preference-based orders. Overparenting, your child could have disastrous consequences.

Awful Directions

The words used to command are quite important. "Please clean your teeth at this time," suggests a choice. Please pick up your toys quickly. These directives make you sound incompetently authoritative. Clarify your commands and avoid requesting favors from your children.

Can you recite your regulations and rules?

Your youngster will learn not to listen the first time you speak if you nag. He will observe that you repeat yourself frequently and that there is no reason to listen the first time. Don't permit your child to disregard or delay your directives.

You enforce consequences.

If you instruct your child to clean his teeth but do nothing when he does not, he will learn to ignore you. "I will not tell you again to brush your teeth." is unhelpful as well. If your child disregards a warning, demonstrate the repercussions. Allow him to use electronic devices for the day or require him to go to bed early, but ensure that the punishment will motivate him to obey you in the future.

You provide affirmative feedback.

If your youngster does not receive positive attention and reinforcement, he may lose motivation. Despite the importance of positive reinforcement, you do not need to reward your child for every activity, such as placing the dishes in the sink.

Strategy #10 - Anger Management Lessons

Demonstrate acceptable anger management techniques.

It is essential to teach your children how to effectively manage their emotions. Display your emotional management skills while you're angry. Apologize and discuss what you could have done instead of raising your voice in the first place. Accept individual responsibility for your actions.

To Establish Anger Rules

The majority of families have unofficial norms for dealing with rage and anger. Some families are tolerant of loud shouting and slamming doors, but others are not. Create a set of home rules. Respect for others should be emphasized in anger rules. Explain to your children that when they are angry, they cannot harm people, destroy property, or verbally or physically attack others.

Teach Effective Adaptation Skills.

Children must learn the appropriate means of expressing disapproval. Instead of lecturing them not to strike their siblings, teach them what to do when they are frustrated. "Use your words the next time," or "When you're angry, go away." In addition, you may ask, "What else could you do instead of a strike?" to help your youngster consider alternative actions.

In addition, you might consider creating a calm-down kit for them to use if they become agitated. Prepare a box of treats, such as a coloring book and crayons, scented lotion, and soothing music, to help them unwind. By engaging their senses, individuals can help calm their minds and bodies. Utilize a timeout to help your child calm down. Teach children to take a break prior to engaging in mischief. For children prone to anger, withdrawing from a situation and taking a few moments to calm down can be highly therapeutic. In addition, teach youngsters problem-solving skills so that they realize they may resolve issues without resorting to violence. Discuss peaceful methods of dispute resolution.

Provide consequences when required.

Give your children consequences for violating the anger rules and rewards for following them. A reward or token economy system can be used to teach a child how to control their anger. For instance, timeouts, a reduction or loss of privileges, or compensating activities such as donating a toy to the person who was harmed by their violence can be helpful methods for getting children to stop being aggressive.

Strategy #11 - Delivering Negative Repercussions

If you intend to apply negative consequences, ensure that they are effective. For instance, if your teen watches television shows online, removing the television will not be effective. Removing a child's access to television may be upsetting to some but not to others. Your child's punishments should be tailored to their specific requirements. Here are some potential undesirable outcomes:

- The logical consequences of inappropriate behavior are directly related. For instance, you could take your child's bicycle away if he makes a poor decision with it.
- Ignoring your child's attention-grabbing behavior, such as throwing a tantrum, may be the most effective kind of negative punishment.
- Placing your children in a brief timeout may assist them in avoiding future misbehavior.
- The assignment of additional responsibilities can have a positive effect.

Avoid Rewarding Bad Behavior

Unwittingly, parents might foster negative behavior in their children. This can, unfortunately, exacerbate existing behavioral disorders. When you tell a child to "stop whining" or encourage a finicky eater to "eat just one more bite," you may be rewarding undesired behaviors. Even negative attention can be an effective reinforcer. Therefore, you should recognize excellent conduct while overlooking small transgressions. Your child should be disciplined for rule-breaking.

Strategy #12 - Delayed Gratification

Delaying gratification is a form of self-discipline that can yield long-term benefits. Imagine, for instance, that your child has a final project due in social studies. If he receives just Bs and As in class, you have committed to taking him to his favorite restaurant for supper.

However, tonight is the airing of your child's favorite program, and he plans to watch it. His work will suffer if he watches television programs. This is known to him. Do you want your youngster to select between an immediate incentive (viewing television) and a later reward (dinner)? The issue at hand is your child's ability to deal with delayed gratification.

Another instance of delayed gratification is determining whether to spend now or save for the future. A new bicycle may be exactly what your child desires. He has saved enough money to purchase a cheap bicycle that they do not desire. Additionally, your child can continue saving for their dream bicycle.

From childhood to adolescence, the capacity to withhold gratification develops. People tend to internalize the concept of delayed gratification in late adolescence. Frequently, a parent or other adult must assist a child in choosing the higher incentive over the more immediate and modest reward. Parenting children who have difficulty with delayed gratification can be difficult.

With a few simple tactics, you may help your child postpone pleasure. Together with your child, create a plan for accomplishing the objective to guarantee that your child has a path to success. You may decide to create a tracking calendar for your child or establish goals that can be observed and evaluated. Offering your child moral and emotional support while he completes the assignment will have a positive impact.

You should keep the promises you make to your child.

If your child's arithmetic grades improve, make good on your promise to take them to the movies. Your child will eventually understand that his actions have repercussions. This can assist your youngster in focusing on greater objectives and working to achieve them.

Strategy #13 - The Inventory of Distractions

Check the various areas of the home for activities that might be too stimulating for a child, such as the presence of music or the television during mealtimes or while they are working on their assignments, and clean up any mess that makes it difficult for children to keep their school supplies in order. Children's use of digital gadgets such as cellphones, tablet computers, computers, and other electronic devices, which may be overstimulating them and causing sleep disruptions, should be limited in order to preserve their health and prevent them from developing health problems. Figure out how to use digital technology in a way that is beneficial to both you and your children. It may also be beneficial to have a workstation that faces the wall rather than a window so that they have fewer opportunities for distraction.

Strategy #14 - Beware of Overstimulation

For example, if you sense that your child is becoming agitated or overstimulated, you have the ability to swiftly intervene and have them take a timeout in another room in order to calm down. If you keep an eye out for these telltale signals, it will be much simpler for you to identify situations that can trigger troublesome behavior and steer clear of them in the future. It is critical to have conversations with your child. It can be best to wait until they have calmed down before inquiring about how they are feeling and why they believe they "exploded." Children may have an easier time concentrating on their work or falling asleep if they are in a setting that is quiet and devoid of distractions. It's probably best to keep any electronic gadgets your child uses outside of their bedroom or study space.

Strategy #15 - Favorize a sport or hobby

Parents and children alike frequently come to the realization that physical activity and sports are excellent ways to let off some of the excess energy that they have been storing up. However, it is absolutely necessary to have an adult oversee children's physical activities, as an excessive amount of physical activity might cause some youngsters to become overly excited. When a child has ADHD, they have an increased risk of developing inattention-related injuries. Therefore, certain sports might not be appropriate for them. If you want your youngster to have an easier time falling asleep at night, it is best to engage in physical activities and sports in the afternoon rather than in the evening. Reading and knitting are two other enjoyable activities that might help make life a little less complicated. It is essential for a child to have a passion or activity that they enjoy, as that also gives them the opportunity to be successful, which is essential for them to flourish. When children are made to feel valued and are made aware that they have performed well at something, studies have shown that they are more likely to concentrate on tasks that they are not as enthusiastic about.

Strategy #16 - If things get overwhelming, seek assistance.

In order to counteract the stresses of daily life and retain composure in the face of their child's tantrums, it is essential that parents take care of themselves. They should seek assistance from others, such as friends or family members who can provide a break or a professional who can provide parenting assistance. Consider close friends or family with whom the child gets along well and who can periodically spend time with them without being involved in their day-to-day struggles. Each parent receives a break, which benefits everyone. Participating in parent education programs, seeking advice from ADHD specialists, and establishing trustworthy relationships with these professionals are viewed as tremendously beneficial by many parents.

Being more patient, calm, and tolerant could help you deal with the obstacles of everyday life better. Those who have children with ADHD may benefit from sharing their experiences in a self-help group with other parents. Regardless of the form of assistance you choose, you may make family life much simpler by accepting assistance from others and proactively solving challenges so that you can assist your child in the most effective manner. A brief break can assist with refocusing.

Strategy #17 - Practice Mindfulness

According to specialists, children with ADHD must regularly practice mindfulness. Those who have practiced it describe it as an intentional awareness process, a judgment-free blossoming from one moment to the next. Before the start of ADHD symptoms, children should be instructed in mindfulness. Mindfulness-based cognitive therapy, in contrast to cognitive behavioral therapy, encourages patients to pay attention to their thoughts without judging them. Body scanning may be included in mindfulness practice. Performing a mental scan of one's own body in this manner enables the observer to identify sensations in various sections of it. It is conceivable for a youngster or an adult to realize that their legs are aching or their shoulders are stiff after engaging in this exercise. People who practice this sort of self-observation do not judge themselves or suppress their emotions. The individual can next direct efforts toward implementing improvements.

Strategy #18 - Get a Pet

The notions of personal responsibility and empathy, which can be taught through animals, may be challenging for some children who have ADHD. Children who have ADHD may find relief from their anxiety and excess energy through engaging in activities such as walking their dogs or cuddling. For instance, providing sustenance is a job that calls for a significant amount of prior planning. They might be able to more effectively manage their time if they did this.

Chapter 11
Strategies to Manage ADHD Behaviors (Part 2)

Strategy #19 - Give Them the School Tools

- A digital school calendar: After-school activities and social engagements should have their own calendar. Everything may be added to a digital calendar with a reminder feature that delivers push notifications to the phone, which makes it easy to keep track of everything. This enables his parents and instructors to view his daily schedule.

- Students with ADHD can stay on top of their studies by sitting in the front row of the classroom. The more difficult it is for children with ADHD to fall through the cracks, the better.

- Give him a set of highlighters and label each one with a "priority level," such as "high," "medium," and "low," with "pink" representing the highest importance. Having a structure in place will facilitate his learning of the process's specifics. Apps such as "Remember the Milk" provide rough estimates of how long each task will take.

- Children can enhance their ability to estimate how long each task will take and when it is time to move on to the next one by using timers. Using a timer can also help him remember to switch segments and maximize his time on lengthier examinations.

- Planned play dates can help a child with ADHD who has difficulty making and keeping friends because she does not know how to communicate with others. With scheduled playdates, you can instruct your son and help him overcome his anxiety about interacting with other children who share his condition.

- Prior to the beginning of the school year, children who stopped taking their medications during the summer should resume doing so. It is essential to monitor the timetable throughout the day (even in the mornings!) and adjust it so that children do not crash at the end of the day or suffer math meltdowns in the afternoon.

- If students want to excel in the classroom, they must pay attention to lectures and verbal instructions, regardless of their individual demands. The use of recording software with dictation capabilities will help students organize their work. He will be able to catch up on all he missed.

Strategy #20 - Develop a Functional Study Space

Workplace circumstances must be conducive to comfort. To accomplish this, place your child's or teen's legs on a chair. Sitting at a desk or on their lap is optimal for focus, but they should choose what works best for them. Utilizing a recliner or cushioned chair might make it feasible to concentrate for extended periods of time while sitting comfortably.

Reduce the number of interruptions. Your children will benefit from less frequent switching between books and computers, documents on computers, and getting up to fetch supplies. Many individuals benefit from using a laptop with an external display (e.g., an LCD television). They are able to keep a reference document open while writing. In addition, the tablet can be utilized as a laptop stand. In the kitchen, it can be beneficial to keep textbooks open in a book holder. Keep an assortment of writing implements on hand for your children's education.

The environment's visual and auditory cacophony is being diminished. If you find a window distracting, face the workstation away from it. Using a white noise generator or app to reduce background noise is an excellent way to concentrate without being distracted (with or without headphones).

Strategy #21 - Get Help from their Teachers

It is vital to stock up on essentials such as pencils and pens, in addition to a variety of additional tools such as rulers and clipboards. Help your youngster organize his supplies by labeling the desk, desk drawers, or table drawers.

Establish a system with your child's teacher for keeping track of assignments. This documentation will be sent home with your kid from school. This notebook/folder should contain a calendar or planner for longer-term assignments and tests. Look at this calendar with your child. Use the calendar to help your child divide up larger projects. Consider that you and your child may need to be creative to find a solution.

Request that the teacher remind your child to complete homework assignments in a notebook. This phase ensures that they understand the tasks and record them accurately in a notebook. In addition, the teacher can check your child's book bag at the end of the day to ensure that it contains the correct books, papers, and homework notes.

Request a printed copy of the daily homework assignments for your child's homework notebook if he has difficulty with handwriting. It would be even better if the teacher could provide handouts with three pre-punched holes for easy placement in the homework notebook.

Before the next school day, review your assignments and literature. Supervise your child while he places these items in the backpack and places it near the front door. Now, it is easier to locate the book bag.

Request that the teacher assist your child with organizing and cleaning their school desk and locker. Maintain a regular cleaning regimen for your child's school backpack and notebooks. Recognize that your youngster will require support and supervision. To develop excellent habits, you must assist your child through these steps and have him practice them frequently.

Reserve specific spaces on the desk or locker You can also use tape to "draw" these spots to indicate where notes, books, files, and writing implements should be stored. This will facilitate the relocation of the items.

Invest in a collection of color-coded folders, notebook covers, and book jackets. Color-code your child's assignments. Math is represented by the color red, while language arts are represented by yellow, etc. Share this with the instructor in order for them to assist your child. The instructor can also color-code handouts for each subject.

Create a compelling incentive scheme to encourage your child's development of daily organizational skills.

Strategy #22 - The Categorizing Noun Game

Nouns of the World

- You could play a game with your class where everyone has to answer questions about the current term. An alphabet set plus a separate deck of cards with nouns like "person," "place," "thing," and "idea" are all the instructor needs to play this noun game with his class.

- A contest between two students.

- The teacher selects a card from each pile and reads off the corresponding alphabet and nouns.

- The first student to give the right answer moves behind the other student's desk.

- If a student wins, they move on to compete against the next student.

- Feel free to make changes to suit your class's knowledge base and review requirements. Displaying alphabet flashcards and having students come up with nouns that begin with each letter is a more straightforward alternative.

List the Noun

Create a unique game with a simple list of nouns.

- Get kids to write as many nouns as they can in one or two minutes by drawing a letter on the board.

- Invite a few students to read aloud their lists to the class in order to confirm that proper nouns were included.

Advanced classes can focus on particular types of nouns.

Nouns related to sports

- Separate the class into groups of three to four students. While one student serves as the recorder, the remainder of the class will respond.
- At the beginning of each round, a new sport is announced, and each team is allowed one minute to jot down any terminology they can think of.
- Determine which team has the most nouns after one minute has passed.
- Consider granting bonus points for the use of collective nouns (team, squad, crowd).

You can modify this game by requesting other activity-related grammatical categories in addition to sports.

Strategy #23 - The Morning/After-School Scheduler

Start with your child's routine.

The morning ritual is intended to get everyone ready and out the door on time. It is essential to prepare the night before in order to avoid a chaotic morning. Due to the fact that many children with ADHD are easily distracted, you should minimize distracting stimuli. Such as:

- Turn the television off in the morning.
- Refrain from accessing your computer to check your e-mail.
- Put away the new publication or catalog until after school or later that evening.

Homework Helpers After School

ADHD children are only consistent in their unpredictability. This creates difficulties for cerebral work. Homework, which evaluates a child's ability to self-regulate, requires the most consistency and organization. Parents and children sometimes dispute academics. A study schedule (time, location, and methods) can reduce their frequency and intensity, if not entirely remove them. Adopt a homework routine for increased productivity and academic success.

- Maintain a consistent start time. This will help your youngster establish the routine of completing his homework at the same time every day.
- Maintain an intimate relationship with your child. Children with ADHD are more attentive

when an adult is present or working alongside them.

- Make regular stops. ADHD is characterized by distractibility, restlessness, difficulties maintaining concentration, and a low tolerance for frustration, all of which almost invariably culminate in mental fatigue and boredom. Beneficial are frequent, brief breaks that allow the youngster to roam around.
- Enjoy yourselves after that. When your child knows that a fun activity, such as playing a game or watching television, will follow his schooling, he is more likely to complete it.

Strategy #24 - Check-Ins

Check-Ins are performed every day. Parents of children with ADHD are all too familiar with the following scenario: Do you have any homework today?

"Nope."
"Great! You have until dinner to kill."

The passage of four hours has elapsed. It is currently 9 p.m. You hear a tap-tap at your bedroom door.

"Umm...
Mom, Dad,

I am required to compose three five-sentence paragraphs about the events leading up to World War I. With citations, the assignment is due the following day.

You can avoid this by reviewing your daily planner and all folders on a daily basis. You do it together initially, and this has always been the case. You might even do it for them the first time so they can observe the process. While opening the binder and examining each piece of paper in each pocket may seem like a no-brainer to an adult, this is not the most effective way to check divider folder pockets in a school context. However, a teen with ADHD may not be aware of this. Therefore, you practice the skill with them daily until they can do it on their own, and then you progressively give them more and more responsibility.

Strategy #25 - Simplify and Declutter

Eliminate disorganization and establish new criteria to prevent it throughout the year. Here are the eleven rules:

- Make use of plastic shopping bags.
- Remove old electronic equipment.
- Eliminate all giveaways.
- Do not keep extra bedsheets.
- Donate your unused cleaning supplies.
- Magazines and catalogs
- Donate everything to get rid of clutter.

- Eliminate all outdated publications and catalogs.

Strategy #26 - Hang Up Laminated Lists

The phrase "clean up your room" has varied connotations for various individuals. There is a possibility that your words to your youngster could be taken as "throw everything under their bed." Be explicit in your expectations. Attach a laminated checklist of chores to the back of your child's bedroom door so they can always see it. It is easy for him to follow the checklist you provide and check off each item as he completes it, such as "Clean up your room."

Strategy #27 - Remember Perfection isn't Perfect

Even if you are the world's most organized person, there is always room for growth. The perfect organization is not only unrealistic but also impossible to accomplish. Not because we have trouble organizing, but because we seek perfection as an end in itself, which we know we will never attain. Reducing your expectations is an excellent method for managing ADHD and maintaining a tidy house. We are not proposing that you discard your entire moral code. If you expect your home to be immaculately clean and organized at all times, we're sorry to say you can't. Perfection is a common goal for individuals with ADHD, and it frequently results in failure or difficulty.

Stop before its weight causes you to be crushed. When you have a husband and children, it can be challenging to keep your home organized. It can be difficult to keep track of things when you only have one roommate. Avoid adding to your stress by making organization impossible. Instead, make an attempt to keep things organized to the best of your ability, and don't get too upset if they occasionally become disorderly.

Strategy #28 - Use a Soft & Calming Tone

Communicating with an ADHD child can be challenging for parents. It can be challenging to convince children to calm down, focus, and comply with directions. ADHD is characterized by a brain that is hyperactive. Imagine your child's brain as a metropolis, with streets delivering information, impulses, sensory input, teacher lectures, and your good parenting advice. Your role as a pillar of stability in your child's life is crucial at challenging times. Regardless of how chaotic their world appears, remember that you are in charge, and everything will be OK. Additionally, they must comprehend that you are emotionally immune to their frenzied outbursts. Color with crayons, peruse a magazine, water your plants, or prepare a delectable meal. Invite him to share in your serenity. Because he is accustomed to seeing you in an agitated state, he will initially be wary of this. You are claiming that I am immune to your control or manipulation. Regardless of how out of control you feel, you can rely on me as a rock.

Strategy #29 - Feeling Charades

Feeling Charades

Each student will need a pack of three 3x5 index cards. On each of the cards, write a feeling. Try to maintain a balance between "positive" and "negative" feelings (excitement, pride, elation, anger, rage, and anxiety). Avoid using the simplest, most commonplace language possible (sad, happy, mad).

Class discussion regarding the significance of expressing one's emotions

To assist children in comprehending the significance of positively expressing their emotions, you may begin the exercise by discussing the significance of understanding the emotions of people around us. More often than not, a person's facial expressions and body language reveal more about their emotions than their words. Today, we will be assessed on our ability to interpret someone's emotions in this manner. During "Feelings Charades," students will have the opportunity to demonstrate one emotion, from which the rest of the class will be able to discern the individual's state of mind. The person taking part in the charade is unable to speak, so they must use their facial expressions and body language to get their peers to do what they want. After the game, the entire class will discuss what transpired.

Select Scribes

Offer your services as "scribes" for the following tasks: If your class has more than 20 to 25 students, divide it into two sections with two scribes per section. While the plays are being played, the scribes will take turns recording the children's reactions and documenting their observations. They will each take turns taking notes. The game of charades is open to everyone who is not taking notes. Inform the scribes that their notes will be used by the class once the charades have been completed.

Demonstrate a Charade

To create a slapstick comedy, use whatever emotion you like. Place your hands in front of your face as if you were using a curtain to cover your face from the sun. Once your hands have crossed your chin, demonstrate emotion. Observe the kids' emotions and allow them to guess your meaning. If they do not receive it within one minute, inform them.

Class Charades

Ensure that each child can perform charades or locate volunteers. Request that each performer choose a card. And just facial expressions and body language should demonstrate their speech. Confirm that they comprehend and can perform their duties. Rush till everyone has acted.

Strategy #30 - Guess What Happens Next

A player begins the game by telling a story. Occasionally, they ask listeners (or viewers), "Guess what's coming next?" Whatever they say is universally acknowledged as being absolutely accurate. It is included in the story, and the story continues.

Playing Guidelines

- Organize everyone into pairs. One person begins by sharing a story with the other.
- Occasionally, the storyteller will pause and ask the audience to predict what will happen next.
- After the audience member makes a guess, the narrator exclaims with delight, "Exact!"
- "The narrator uses the audience's observations to continue the story.
- Continue for however long it is desired. Alter the roles of the participants and have them play again.

Strategy #31- Plastic Egg Faces – Teaching Emotions

You will need

- Plastic eggs that break in half
- Permanent marker
- Modeling clay (optional)

It began by doodling different facial expressions on each plastic egg. Some appeared to be happy, some sad, others angry, and still others proud. Insert modeling clay into the bottom of each egg to prevent it from standing upright (or bobbing). Emotional eggs are wonderful because they may be shattered and combined to produce a variety of unique emotions. The only ways to significantly alter a person's face are by altering the form of their eyes or the position of their mouth. The "emotion" feature on your iPhone is an excellent source of inspiration for eye and lip shapes.

Strategy #32 - The Mood Meter

https://www.teacherspayteachers.com/Product/Emoji-Mood-Meter-Social-Emotional-Learning-Classroom-Management-3999890

The integration of the mood meter into a kindergarten classroom could not be simpler. The emojis are suitable for children of all ages, and there are sufficient possibilities for them to express their emotions without feeling overwhelmed. The teachers welcomed this positively. This strategy allows teachers to better comprehend the ideas and emotions of their students. Teachers have utilized it frequently in the classroom to determine the emotional state of their students and whether or not they can manage their emotions to be more ready to learn.

Strategy #33 - Use Nonverbal Communication Cues

Body language, facial emotions, and gestures all contribute to the potential for efficient interpersonal communication. A youngster with ADHD may miss nonverbal cues, such as a shift in voice tone or the plethora of emotions spoken without words. For instance, a child with ADHD may approach a stranger even closer if he fails to recognize the negative reaction he is receiving from the other child's facial expression. Similarly, children with ADHD struggle to respond when a parent or teacher adjusts their tone of voice. Effective communication entails recognizing and reacting appropriately to these nonverbal clues. Sadly, children with ADHD frequently miss these indications. When their classmates and teachers lose patience with their excessive impulsivity, they are left wondering what happened.

Strategy #34 - Expression Through Writing

There is a reason why your child may occasionally appear to be mute. Children with ADHD or a learning handicap typically lag behind their peers in linguistic skills. Children with ADHD have difficulty comprehending what they hear and putting their thoughts into phrases. Even when they know the answer, they cannot respond quickly to a teacher's questions. Additionally, textual communication is more difficult. Creating new ideas, recalling memories, and sticking to spelling and grammar standards may make it more challenging for students with ADHD to complete their classwork and exams on time. Inadequate fine motor skills can also impede writing and detract focus from tasks.

Solutions

In the Classroom

- When giving information, speak slowly and in small segments.
- Make it easier for children with ADHD to participate in the discussion.
- Permit students who struggle with verbal expression to submit their responses in writing.
- Make it possible for a child with slow handwriting to share a classmate's notes.
- By shortening written assignments and exams, you can lower the amount of time allotted for their completion.
- Do not subtract points for sloppy writing or grammatical errors.
- Refer to the handwriting of a student as an indicator of a learning issue.
- Teach students the art of visual reasoning.
- Discover how to use "self-questioning" as a writing technique.

- Encourage children to demonstrate their understanding of a subject using their individual abilities.

At Home

- Encourage your child's development of a sense of self-expression at home.
- Provide access to literature, film, video games, and software.
- Facilitate your child's participation in the discourse by granting him permission to do so
- Make sure your child is surrounded by loved ones.
- Let me know if you need assistance with your academics, I will assist you.

Strategy #35 - Practice Turn-Taking

Sharing a beloved item is similar to taking turns speaking, and children must learn to do so. The coloring circle is an enjoyable exercise for this age range. At the center of the circle, each youngster may talk about a topic of his choosing. Take the color yellow, for example. The child would have 15 seconds to name all of the yellow hues in their environment. Then, the next youngster in the center chooses a color, and so on. Lastly, the previous person must share two items that each new participant has already heard. It is in our instinct to express our individual identities. The desire to comprehend your child's thoughts and feelings is understandable. It is frustrating when you cannot communicate with your child.

Chapter 12
ADHD in the Schoolyard

Strategy #36 - Plan Ahead with their Teachers

If you wish to speak with school administrators or instructors before the start of the school year, you can make arrangements in advance. If the school year has already begun, schedule at least one monthly meeting with a teacher or counselor.

Meet the Instructors

Pick a time that is convenient for you and your child's teacher, and stick to it. If at all possible, arrange to see your child's classroom before the meeting so that you may get a sense of the physical space in which they will be studying.

Establish a Set of Goals

Create a list of goals for your child with their instructor. First, discuss your goals for your child's academic development. Then, construct a list of attainable goals with your child and explore how you might assist him in achieving them.

Attend closely to the instructors.

Your child's instructor shares your worry about his academic progress. Pay attention to what they are saying, despite the fact that it may be difficult to hear them. Understanding your child's school issues is vital to finding effective solutions for him.

Be Sincere and Share information.

The information should be shared with others. Together, you and your child's teacher have access to a wealth of information that can help you understand your child's problems. Inspire your child's teachers to do the same, and provide them with your observations.

Strategy #37 - Make Distractions Scarce

It is normal for kids with ADHD to miss vital instructional materials due to their inability to concentrate on the current task. It is difficult for these children to maintain concentration on mentally demanding tasks. Therefore, even if they appear attentive, they are not genuinely absorbing what you say. Children who are easily distracted can benefit from physical placement, increased physical exercise, and the division of lengthy tasks into small portions.

- Children with ADHD should not sit near doors or windows. While the student is working, pets should be isolated in another room or corner.

- Alternate activities require the child to remain seated with those requiring movement throughout the room. Whenever possible, physical movement should be incorporated into instruction.
- Important information should be written down and kept in a place where the child can easily find and read it. Give the student a gentle nudge in the direction of the resource.
- Divide huge jobs into smaller tasks and provide youngsters with frequent pauses.

Strategy #38 - Reduce Classroom Interruptions

Children with ADHD frequently struggle to control their impulsive behavior and thus speak out of turn. They regularly interrupt others by shouting or commenting on what they hear in the classroom or at home. As a result of their outbursts being viewed as unfriendly or nasty, they may have social issues. Children with ADHD have low self-esteem, and calling attention to their condition in class or in front of their parents might worsen the situation. When correcting the disruptions of children with ADHD, especially in public, care should be used to safeguard their self-esteem. Employ a "secret language" while communicating with the ADHD child. Agreed-upon gestures or words should be used to let the child know they are interrupting. If the child does not interrupt you, commend him.

Strategy #39 - The Written Behavior Plan

Children with ADHD require school discipline and clear expectations to prevent their symptoms from becoming unmanageable. If you are a parent, you can assist your child by drafting and enforcing a behavioral plan. If you choose to use a behavior plan, collaborate with your child and his teacher to create it. For children with ADHD, well-defined goals, consistent positive reinforcement, and rewarding incentives are most effective. To encourage your youngster to behave better in class, you may need to suspend a carrot from a pole. Create a reward system that acknowledges both minor and significant accomplishments.

Strategy #40 - Keep Expectations Consistent

The classroom rules should be straightforward and unambiguous. Rules and expectations for the class should be reviewed and amended as necessary on a regular basis. Classroom rules should be prominently displayed. Ask your child to repeat what you've just said if you want to ensure they comprehend. Consider the possibility that a child heard you but misunderstood what you said. Students who have trouble managing their time or "shifting gears" from one assignment or class to the next can benefit from keeping their schedules close at hand and reviewing them frequently to facilitate the transition. Using timers, taped signals, or verbal cues can also assist students in determining how much time remains for a certain assignment.

Strategy #41 - Vocabulary Charades

Overview and Purpose: In addition, students will have the opportunity to explore new vocabulary words. Students are required to provide explanations for the meanings of the words they are studying.

Objective: The student will have the following abilities:

- Decipher the vocabulary term acted out by another student.
- Without speaking, demonstrate a vocabulary term so that your classmates can guess it.

Resources: Several props are roughly matched to language phrases.

Activities: For this exercise, students should be divided into pairs or groups of three. Assign each group a vocabulary term, then instruct them to perform it. They are unable to articulate themselves vocally or give a written definition of the term. Give them time to consider how they will convey it. Next, choose a group to perform their script in front of the entire class. The group that correctly guesses the phrase receives a point. You can deduct a point for each incorrect guess to discourage groups from shouting random words.

Closure: It is possible to improve mnemonics by associating a specific activity with a word. Drawing two more ways to act out the vocabulary terms at home could further assist children in reviewing the words at home. The next day, provide them with an opportunity to perform the lines in front of the class.

Strategy #42 - The Homework Routine

- After school, like the majority of children with ADHD do, allow at least 30 minutes to an hour of free time for playing or watching television.
- Establish a consistent location and time for completing assignments.
- Before beginning schoolwork, provide the child with a 10-minute warning.
- Children require assistance in reviewing the job and ensuring that they have the necessary materials.
- Allow the youngster to take brief breaks as needed. Getting up and moving around for a few minutes can do wonders for mental clarity and reduce uneasiness. However, maintain vigilance and be prepared to divert the child's focus or answer inquiries.
- Not only should the results be praised, but also the efforts. Perform regularly!
- Verify the task's completion.

- Gather all homework and school resources required for the following day. Everything must be placed in the backpack and stored at the entrance door.
- After schoolwork is complete, enjoy a fun and relaxing activity together.

Strategy #43 - Use a Home-School Communication Tracker

Each student's tracker can be adapted to their individual requirements. Your child's demands can be satisfied by designing an age-appropriate and interest-specific tracker in collaboration with a teacher. Consider the following points when deploying a tracker:

- Concentrate on the positives. Don't penalize habits that require improvement by rewarding positive conduct.
- Focus on two to five key habits. Your child will become overwhelmed if you list an excessive number of behaviors at once.
- Plan rewards for progress and accomplishment on the trackers you've created. Every day after school, rewards should be useful, motivating, and easily available. Determine what inspires your child, not just what you consider to be the best course of action. If the reward is associated with the behavior, it will be more effective. For example, if your child regularly completes their

schoolwork on time, you could express gratitude.

- They can quickly liberate time to engage in enjoyable pursuits. Being responsible can allow children to engage in activities that require greater maturity, such as staying up later if they so choose.

- Regularly check the status of the tracker. Then, if possible, adapt to your child's evolving abilities and needs. Next, work on the tracker with your child and his teacher. Reward modifications should be made.

There are several actions that could be tracked, including:

- Homework submissions
- Appropriately gains the teacher's attention.
- Attends class on time.
- Arrives to class well-prepared.
- Waited patiently for his turn to speak.
- Exhibits respect for the instructor and fellow students.
- Complies with directives.
- Adheres to the rules
- Maintains focus
- Assignments are completed
- Remains in place.

- Keeps one's hands and feet to oneself.
- Works in silence.

Learning might be difficult for a student with ADHD. In addition, if this is one of the symptoms, your child will not be able to focus as well as other youngsters. With the assistance of teachers and these tactics, it is possible to effectively manage your child's education.

Chapter 13
Tips for Parents on How to Take Care of Themselves

Tips for parents of children with ADHD on how to care for themselves

There are ways to take care of yourself so that you can continue being a fantastic parent on a daily basis, even if a trip to the spa isn't always possible.

Positive self-talk

Teaching your child good manners is just as important as encouraging positive self-talk. You are a fantastic parent if you persist in raising a child with ADHD despite the numerous frustrating moments. You have the right to receive encouragement and assistance during times of difficulty. Isn't it a lot simpler to tell a friend going through a tough time all the good things about them, but we rarely do the same for ourselves? Beneficial self-talk has a positive effect on our attitude and outlook on the day, which has a ripple effect on others around us.

Reasonable Expectations

The level of expectations we place on ourselves and those around us can occasionally lead to stress. Parenting is all about allowing your child to learn and develop at his own pace. You will gain a better understanding of your child's growth if you set acceptable expectations for his current and future levels. Setting reasonable expectations for your child's home, education, and overall development will alleviate the stress of unfulfilled expectations. The realistic expectations that you set for your child may be difficult, but they are also attainable.

Set reachable expectations for your child, but also ensure that your own standards are reasonable. Everyone wants to be superhuman, but it is essential that we give our bodies, minds, and souls a vacation from time to time. To offer the best care possible for your child, you must first prioritize your own health. This could involve asking for assistance, canceling activities, or just saying "no."

Suggestions for Parents of Children with ADHD Regarding Self-Care

- You and your partner should maintain open lines of communication. It is essential that you and your partner raise your children as a team. It is preferable to support one another because neither parent is responsible for their child's disability.

- Boost your self-esteem by expressing positive things about yourself. By doing so, you can act as a role model for your child. Parents can demonstrate to their children that they can see the good in themselves despite their shortcomings by praising themselves.

- Every day, remind yourself that your child did not choose to suffer from ADHD.

- You are not a bad parent, and you never will be.

- Display a copy of the prayer for serenity in your home. While we may wish to alter certain aspects of life, we must learn to accept those we cannot alter.

- Every day, do something enjoyable for yourself to improve your mood. You deserve it. Walk, do some yoga, or read a book. Take some time to unwind.

- Search the area for anything amusing or humorous. You can do this for yourself or with your child to maintain a lighthearted atmosphere. It is possible to enjoy yourself while laughing at the antics of a loved one.

- Make light of all situations.

- Reflect upon your day. Take pride in all of your achievements.

- Trying to be the perfect parent is futile. No perfect parents exist. You can only hope for success if you do your absolute best.

- Discuss your feelings and concerns with a friend or therapist who is kind and nonjudgmental. If you ever find yourself in a difficult circumstance and in need of someone to talk to, consider this resource. It's possible that you'll need it eventually.

- Find a support group for those with ADHD. If you have an issue or a victory to share with your child, this is a fantastic method.

- Exercise a minimum of three times per week. This practice will enhance both your emotional and physical health. This may be a technique for couples to manage their stress levels together.

- Delegate domestic responsibilities to family members.

- Utilize ways of bettering one's own conduct. Use these tactics if you need to modify a negative behavior in a child with ADHD.

- Utilize the assistance provided. Instead of self-medicating with narcotics or prescription pharmaceuticals, if you are sad or worried, you should seek the assistance of a mental health professional. People that work with ADHD patients may have extensive knowledge of the disorder and be able to provide additional assistance.

- Make it a point to commend your child's accomplishments.
- Be honest with yourself.

These are some strategies to make it easier to parent an ADHD child. Depression in adolescents is notoriously difficult to treat. If you are a parent, it is essential that you take care of yourself during this time in your life.

Affirmations

These Affirmations Are Crucial for Emotionally Exhausted Mothers!

- In my opinion, the only person who can bring me down is myself.
- I am treasured.
- I am capable of tremendous feats.
- My family is always by my side.
- Each day has a purpose, and that purpose is to share God's love with others.
- I am the ideal mother for my kids.
- Even in the midst of the turmoil, my home is filled with love and joy.
- I am not flawless, but I was never intended to be.
- I am in charge of my own life, not vice versa.
- I am able to forgive myself and others for our mistakes.

- I am solely responsible for my own well-being.
- Daily, I develop as a mother and as a person.
- Without remorse, I vow to live each day to its fullest extent.
- To achieve success, I must accept responsibility for my actions.
- I am satisfied.
- I make all of the decisions.
- I can rely on my own discretion.
- I consider everyone's interests and needs to be of equal importance.
- It makes no difference what others think.
- A joyful mother raises a joyful family.
- It's OK to take some time for yourself.
- There is a pattern or explanation for the errors we make. Gaining knowledge from them is a plus.
- I am able to offer my children a happy mother.
- It is my obligation as a parent to demonstrate healthy conduct for my children.
- I prioritize my personal health in order to best help others.
- Not everything that I am, but a substantial portion of who I am.
- Instead of stressing about little matters, I will focus on making memories that will last a lifetime.
- Do not settle for less from others.

- Cherished mothers are not flawless mothers.
- Just as the harshest judgments emanate from within, so do the kindest assessments
- There is no purpose in dwelling on the past.
- Even though tomorrow has not yet arrived, Nonetheless, things may change.
- I'm a better person because I've had to overcome obstacles and make mistakes.
- Even if I cannot comprehend why something occurs, there is always an explanation.
- My self-esteem is hurting as a result of my tendency to compare myself to others. Each person is a one-of-a-kind creation.
- Despite my flaws and weaknesses, I love and accept myself as a complete individual.
- I will not share with myself any information that I would not share with my child.

Top self-care suggestions for parents of ADHD children

The importance of sleep

It is essential to keep in mind that proper sleep can give you the appearance of having more time. You may desire to do "just one more thing" or delay going to bed. You'll have greater energy if you get a good night's sleep, which you'll need if you have a child with ADHD in order to handle daily problems. Determine the amount of sleep you require to feel your best. The normal recommended sleep duration in the United States is between seven and nine hours per night. Determine what time of day you need to wake up first. Give yourself an extra hour or more each night to wind down and get ready for bed by setting your alarm 30 minutes earlier than usual. Establishing a pattern that incorporates dark lighting, calming music, and bedtime stories is an excellent way to convince the whole family to relax before bed.

Meditation

Emotional and physical weariness are the norm while raising a child with ADHD! You may become frustrated, furious, or impatient when your children fail to meet your expectations. If you fail to live up to your own expectations as a parent, you may experience significant shame. Meditation is an effective tool. Take a few minutes to meditate if you are feeling overwhelmed, emotional, or reactive in your everyday life. This will assist you in becoming calmer and more attentive around children.

By practicing mindfulness and focusing solely on the present, you can enhance your ability to be present and aware. Meditation can provide us with a gap between recognizing our thoughts and feelings and reacting to them. During that pause, you have the option to select your response or reaction. As a result of this practice, we can learn to observe our thoughts and emotions without quickly reacting to them. When you take a breath, you can respond with compassion and composure.

Use Mantras

The following are some soothing mantras for parents:

- As long as this is not an emergency, I can manage it.
- It seems as though I inhale love and exhale peace.
- It would be wonderful if my child could attend school.
- Behavior is a means of communication.
- Thank you, God, for caring for me.
- I currently have all I could possibly require.

Breathe!

Specific respiratory workouts

- Inhale five times, hold your breath for seven seconds, then exhale eight times. Rather than counting, regularly observe whether your exhales are longer than your inhales.
- This technique entails inhaling for four breaths, holding for four breaths, and then exhaling for four breaths, likewise holding for four breaths. As you count to four, you can use your finger to draw a box or square.

- Inhale as you mentally repeat the mantra, and then exhale as you mentally complete the passage.
- Make an attempt to connect your thoughts to your breath.
- A deeper state of relaxation and healing might result from filling your head with happy thoughts.

When Should Breathing Exercises Be Performed?

These places are good for concentrating on calm, deep breaths:

- Whether you're the driver or a passenger, it's important to be safe.
- If you're rocking a baby or young child, do so gently.
- Nursing a baby
- Keep an eye out for children in the car.

Do a Body Scan

The following areas of your body should receive special attention in this manner:

- Toes → ball of the foot
- Calves → quads
- Stomach
- Mind
- Heart

Keeping things stuffed will just exacerbate your anxiety, which will inevitably explode. Instead, focus on how you feel across your entire body to help remove any stress.

Savor

- Focus on the positive aspects of each of your five senses to relish them.
- What you see around you—what you appreciate in nature, your family's harmony, and the fortunate home you may call your own.
- What you hear: the sounds of food frying, birds singing, the rustle of foliage, and music.
- What you smell: You appreciate essential oils, your hair, perfume, and your baby's soft skin.
- How you felt in the past: Recall good memories from your past. Journaling is an excellent way to appreciate the present.
- What you feel: a person or object that is soft or cuddly
- What you taste: Consider the taste, texture, and temperature of the food.

Take a break

Include "silent time" in your agenda. For the duration of a challenging phase, it is prudent to set a daily recharging time. There are many benefits to establishing a break time:

- Taking a break from parenting enables you to be at your best while interacting with your children.
- One of the most important reasons for students to be creative is to have fun on their own.
- A crucial component of a healthy connection is demonstrating to children that being close and loving does not require constant proximity.

The Family Priority Exercise

Try this activity to help your family set their own priorities:

- Set aside at least one hour for family members to sit down and converse.

- Ask each family member to list three things the family should or should not prioritize. Such topics as honesty, support, and health should be discussed. Explain that this is not about what you would like to accomplish for yourself but rather what you believe the family should do together.

- Each participant should then "show and tell," disclosing his list and explaining why he chose the items on it.

- Wait until everyone has shared their list before making any comments. Is there a common point of agreement among family members? Is there anything you have overlooked? Do any family members appear reluctant to embrace your new priorities? Instead of criticizing them, tell them you'd rather hear what they should be doing more than their priorities. They still have the opportunity to join in the future.

- Being overwhelmed can have a negative impact on a person's well-being. When you're under a lot of pressure, you could do or say things you later regret. In order to stay out of this predicament, you must prioritize your own needs over the needs of those around you. A parent isn't just someone who loves their child; they are someone who has their own flaws, too.

Conclusion

ADHD is quite widespread. ADHD is more commonly diagnosed in boys than in girls. This is probably owing to differences in the manifestation of ADHD symptoms between the sexes. Boys are stereotypically blamed for suffering from ADHD. The likelihood of unequal sex vulnerability to the illness is actually rather high. Nevertheless, it is commonly thought of as a condition that primarily affects boys due to the fact that some boys may be more prone to displaying the associated behavioral signs. When it comes to managing ADHD, girls have been found to have weaker self-efficacy and poorer coping skills than boys. These differences, however, appear to disappear by adulthood. Boys with this illness are less likely to engage in self-deprecating conduct than girls with it. Similarly, studies have shown that girls are more likely to be profoundly affected by adverse life events than boys are.

Research suggests that while girls may be more likely to display signs of melancholy and anxiety, boys are more likely to demonstrate outwardly manifesting symptoms like violence. Boys with ADHD who act in this way are more likely to be labeled as troublemakers in a variety of settings. The American Psychiatric Association estimates that 8.4 percent of children and 2.5 percent of adults are affected by ADHD. The prevalence of

ADHD diagnoses in boys is higher than in girls. ADHD is diagnosed around three times as often in boys as in girls. Whenever a youngster of school age causes a disturbance in the classroom, a diagnosis is often given. An individual's style of thinking, feeling, and acting can all be impacted by ADHD. This issue can make it hard to maintain concentration for long periods of time or remember details, making it challenging to do activities like homework. Boys who have been diagnosed with ADHD may exhibit more agitation, impulsivity, and heightened levels of activity than their peers. They may also experience learning deficits, trouble focusing, and trouble sitting still in class.

You have my utmost gratitude for reading this book, since the more parents know about ADHD, the more we can do to empower our children and make them proud of who they are. People who don't understand ADHD will always be out there, and while it may be easy to simply say "mind your own business," we have a responsibility to educate ourselves and be prepared to answer comments or queries with understanding, grace, and authority. If we can help people realize how we can work together to help these youngsters achieve, we are the ambassadors of ADHD. To help our children's teachers understand our children, we can use this information. It is even possible for us to request "a compassionate teacher who knows ADHD" each year. The more people we involve in our child's life, the stronger the support system he will have at home. This is your time to shine. Being a parent or caregiver can be tremendously challenging when you have a child with ADHD. In order to succeed, you have to put in the time and effort. Trying to get help from people who don't understand our child's unique combination of needs and challenges can be difficult when those needs and concerns evolve over time. The strain is too much to bear. For this reason, getting help for oneself is critical. As a parent of a child with ADHD, I am a firm believer in seeking out a therapist who has experience working with children with special needs. There are also online support groups for parents of children with ADHD, as well as specific Facebook communities for those parents. To be able to help your child, you must first take care of your own needs. When you feel isolated, know that you aren't.

Reference

ADDitude Editors, & Dodson, W., MD. (2022, July 11). What Is ADHD? Attention Deficit Hyperactivity Disorder in Children and Adults. ADDitude. https://www.additudemag.com/what-is-adhd-symptoms-causes-treatments/

Angel, T. (2021, October 13). Everything You Need to Know About ADHD. Healthline. https://www.healthline.com/health/adhd

Attention Deficit Hyperactivity Disorder (ADHD). (2008, September 18). WebMD. https://www.webmd.com/add-adhd/childhood-adhd/attention-deficit-hyperactivity-disorder-adhd

Attention-deficit/hyperactivity disorder (ADHD) in children - Symptoms and causes. (2019, June 25). Mayo Clinic. https://www.mayoclinic.org/diseases-conditions/adhd/symptoms-causes/syc-20350889

CHADD. (2020, October 22). Understanding ADHD https://chadd.org/understanding-adhd/

Team, T. U. (2022, May 4). What is ADHD? John. https://www.understood.org/en/articles/what-is-adhd

ADHD (for Parents) - Nemours KidsHealth. (2020). Lily. https://kidshealth.org/en/parents/adhd.html

NHS website. (2022, January 12). *Attention deficit hyperactivity disorder (ADHD)*. Nhs.Uk. https://www.nhs.uk/conditions/attention-deficit-hyperactivity-disorder-adhd/

Just a moment. . . (2020). Nion. https://www.psychiatry.org/patients-families/adhd/what-is-adhd

Understanding ADHD: Information for Parents. (2020). HealthyChildren.Org. https://www.healthychildren.org/English/health-issues/conditions/adhd/Pages/Understanding-ADHD.aspx

ADHD and school changes. (2022, April 19). Centers for Disease Control and Prevention. https://www.cdc.gov/ncbddd/adhd/features/adhd-and-school-changes.html#:%7E:text=ADHD%20and%20schools&text=This%20can%20mean%20special%20education,organizing%20work%2C%20and%20frequent%20communication.

ADHD in the Classroom | CDC. (2022, April 19). Centers for Disease Control and Prevention. https://www.cdc.gov/ncbddd/adhd/school-success.html

ADHD and School (for Parents) - Nemours KidsHealth. (2020). Anton. https://kidshealth.org/en/parents/adhd-school.html

English, A. M., Peirce, A., & Chua, J. P., MD PhD. (2021, July 13). *Ways to Help Children With ADHD in School.* EverydayHealth.Com. https://www.everydayhealth.com/adhd/adhd-in-school.aspx

ADHD: How to Help Your Child Succeed at School. (2017, April 6). WebMD. https://www.webmd.com/add-adhd/childhood-adhd/adhd-how-to-help-your-child-succeed-at-school

Miller, C. (2022, March 22). *What's ADHD (and What's Not) in the Classroom.* Child Mind Institute. https://childmind.org/article/whats-adhd-and-whats-not-in-the-classroom/

ADDitude Editors. (2021, April 22). *10 Ways We Would Fix the U.S. School System.* ADDitude. https://www.additudemag.com/slideshows/how-can-we-improve-education-for-students-with-adhd/

ADHD Treatment Recommendations | CDC. (2020, February 3). Centers for Disease Control and Prevention. https://www.cdc.gov/ncbddd/adhd/guidelines.html

Guidelines in Practice. (2021, January 15). *Updated guideline on ADHD defines the role of primary care.*

172

https://www.guidelinesinpractice.co.uk/neurology-/updated-guideline-on-adhd-defines-the-role-of-primary-care/454257.article

ADHD in Children and Adolescents. (2020). Alice. https://www.aafp.org/family-physician/patient-care/clinical-recommendations/all-clinical-recommendations/ADHD.html

Managing attention deficit hyperactivity disorder (ADHD) in children and pre-teens. (2021, July 2). Raising Children Network. https://raisingchildren.net.au/school-age/development/adhd/managing-adhd-5-11-years

M. (2022, March 24). *Treatment for Children with ADHD.* HelpGuide.Org. https://www.helpguide.org/articles/add-adhd/treatment-for-childhood-attention-deficit-disorder-adhd.htm

Newmark, S., MD, & Panel, A. A. M. R. (2022, July 11). *The ADHD Diet Plan: Healthy Foods and Supplements for Kids & Adults.* ADDitude. https://www.additudemag.com/adhd-diet-for-kids-food-fix/

Myers, W., & Laube, J., MD. (2018, January 10). *7 Foods to Avoid If Your Child Has ADHD.* EverydayHealth.Com. https://www.everydayhealth.com/adhd-pictures/how-food-can-affect-your-childs-adhd-symptoms.aspx

ADHD Diet and Nutrition. (2008, May 13). WebMD. https://www.webmd.com/add-adhd/adhd-diets

ADHD Diet for Kids: Foods to Eat and Foods to Avoid. (2022, May 10). Verywell Mind. https://www.verywellmind.com/adhd-diet-for-kids-foods-to-eat-and-foods-to-avoid-5225681

Admin, N. (2022, July 7). *ADHD Nutrition: A Healthy Diet for Kids.* The Nourished Child. https://thenourishedchild.com/healthy-adhd-diet-kids/

Pietrangelo, A. (2020, June 17). *Diet Tips and Snack Ideas for Kids with Attention Deficit Hyperactivity Disorder (ADHD).* Healthline.

https://www.healthline.com/health/adhd/diet-tips-snack-ideas

Patwal, S. (2021, September 30). *ADHD Diet For Kids: Foods To Eat And Foods To Avoid.* MomJunction. https://www.momjunction.com/articles/tips-to-provide-diets-for-kids-with-adhd_00773105/

Guildford, A., PhD. (2022, June 6). *ADHD in children: Eating more fruit and vegetables may improve attention.* John. https://www.medicalnewstoday.com/articles/adhd-in-children-eating-more-fruit-and-vegetables-may-improve-attention

Leonard, J. (2019, May 31). *What are the best diets for ADHD?* Nikey. Retrieved 2020, from https://www.medicalnewstoday.com/articles/325352

Borst, H. (2022, July 12). *Everything to eat (and avoid) if you have ADHD.* The Checkup. https://www.singlecare.com/blog/adhd-diet/

Logan, A. C. (2021, May 27). *5 tips to manage ADHD in children.* Mayo Clinic Health System. https://www.mayoclinichealthsystem.org/hometown-health/speaking-of-health/5-tips-to-manage-adhd-in-children

Porter, E. (2018, September 17). *Parenting Tips for ADHD: Do's and Don'ts.* Healthline. https://www.healthline.com/health/adhd/parenting-tips

Crawford, J. (2018, April 25). *Caring for a child with ADHD: 21 tips.* Alice. https://www.medicalnewstoday.com/articles/321621

M. (2022, March 24). *ADHD Parenting Tips.* HelpGuide.Org. https://www.helpguide.org/articles/add-adhd/when-your-child-has-attention-deficit-disorder-adhd.htm

8 Simple School Strategies for Students With ADHD. (2020, June 29). Verywell Mind. https://www.verywellmind.com/help-for-students-with-adhd-20538

The 8 Most Effective Ways to Discipline a Child With ADHD. (2020, May 11). Verywell Family.

https://www.verywellfamily.com/discipline-strategies-for-kids-with-adhd-1094941

NHS website. (2022, June 1). *Living with.* Nhs.Uk. https://www.nhs.uk/conditions/attention-deficit-hyperactivity-disorder-adhd/living-with/

10 strategies for managing children with ADHD in the classroom | *ADHD NZ.* (2022). ADHD NEW ZEALAND. https://www.adhd.org.nz/10-strategies-for-managing-children-with-adhd-in-the-classroom.html

The Royal Children's Hospital Melbourne. (2020). *Kids Health Information : ADHD – ways to help children at school and home.* https://www.rch.org.au/kidsinfo/fact_sheets/ADHD_ways_to_help_children_at_school_and_home/

Children's Health. (2020). *How to manage your child's ADHD at home.* Boardy. https://www.childrens.com/health-wellness/managing-adhd-at-home

ADHD: How to Help Your Child Succeed at School. (2017, April 6). WebMD. https://www.webmd.com/add-adhd/childhood-adhd/adhd-how-to-help-your-child-succeed-at-school

Miller, G. (2021, July 22). *Parenting Kids with ADHD: 12 Tips to Tackle Common Challenges.* Psych Central. https://psychcentral.com/childhood-adhd/parenting-kids-with-adhd-tips-to-tackle-common-challenges

How to Increase Success at Home for Children With ADHD. (2020). Children's Hospital of Philadelphia. https://www.chop.edu/health-resources/how-increase-success-home-children-adhd

CHADD. (2021, June 24). *Parenting a Child with ADHD.* https://chadd.org/for-parents/overview/

Jacobson, R. (2022, July 13). *School Success Kit for Kids With ADHD.* Child Mind Institute. https://childmind.org/article/school-success-kit-for-kids-with-adhd/

Azul Therapy Services. (2021, November 15). *4 Tips to Manage ADHD in Kids.*

https://azultherapyservices.com/blog/4-tips-to-manage-adhd-in-kids/

Sachs, G. P. (2022, February 19). *8 Ways to Deal with ADHD Kids.* wikiHow. https://www.wikihow.com/Deal-with-ADHD-Kids

10 Tips for Parenting a Child With ADHD: Boys vs. Girls. (2022, July 21). eMedicineHealth. https://www.emedicinehealth.com/10_tips_for_parenting_a_child_with_adhd/article_em.htm

Carpenter, D., & Saline, S. P. (2021, May 1). *Never Punish a Child for Bad Behavior Outside Their Control.* ADDitude. https://www.additudemag.com/behavior-punishment-parenting-child-with-adhd/

Guest Author for www.rtor.org. (2021, May 6). *Helping Children with ADHD Focus Without Medication: 7 Tips for Parents.* Resources To Recover. https://www.rtor.org/2021/05/03/helping-children-with-adhd-focus-without-medication-tips-for-parents/

Help Your Child With ADHD | Parents Guide to Support. (2020). YoungMinds. https://www.youngminds.org.uk/parent/parents-a-z-mental-health-guide/adhd/

15 Tips for Helping Your Child With ADHD. (2020). Arthur. https://www.arnoldpalmerhospital.com/content-hub/15-tips-for-helping-your-child-with-adhd

30 Tips on Managing Attention Deficit Disorder (ADD) at Home | HealthyPlace. (2021, December 20). Thomas. https://www.healthyplace.com/adhd/children-behavioral-issues/30-tips-on-managing-attention-deficit-disorder-add-at-home

Team, T. U. (2021, April 20). *ADHD: Ways to help your child at home.* Nancy. https://www.understood.org/en/articles/adhd-strategies-you-can-try-at-home

Centre, A. (2022, June 23). *Great Parenting Tips and Strategies for Coping with ADHD.* The ADHD Centre. https://www.adhdcentre.co.uk/great-parenting-tips-and-strategies-for-coping-with-adhd/

What Can Parents Do to Help Their Child With ADHD? (2021, August 18). MedicineNet. https://www.medicinenet.com/what_can_parents_do_t o_help_their_child_with_adhd/article.htm

Human Performance Resources. (2020). *6 holistic, Total Force Fitness ways to help manage ADHD symptoms in kids.* HPRC. https://www.hprc-online.org/total-force-fitness/tff-strategies/6-holistic-total-force-fitness-ways-help-manage-adhd-symptoms

Collier, E. (2022, June 15). *Managing ADHD in the Classroom: Teaching Strategies and. . .* The Hub | High Speed Training. https://www.highspeedtraining.co.uk/hub/managing-adhd-in-the-classroom/

10 Tips For Coping With A Hyperactive Child. (2017, November 15). EverydayHealth.Com. https://www.everydayhealth.com/emotional-health/adhd/10-tips-coping-with-hyperactive-child/

Revere Health. (2021, April 16). *4 Tips to Manage Your Child's ADHD.* https://reverehealth.com/live-better/4-tips-manage-childs-adhd/

Halliwell, N. (2022, July 1). *Top tips: ADHD in children and young people.* Guidelines in Practice. https://www.guidelinesinpractice.co.uk/mental-health/top-tips-adhd-in-children-and-young-people/456106.article

A. (2022, May 19). *Strategies for Adults Living With ADHD.* Advanced Psychiatry Associates. https://advancedpsychiatryassociates.com/resources/bl og/strategies-for-adults-living-with-adhd/